365 DAYS OF

KAWAii

How to Draw Cute Stuff Every Day of the Year

MAYUMI JEZEWSKI

EASY STEP-BY-STEP DRAWING

DAVID & CHARLES

www.davidandcharles.com

KAWAII DRAWING SECRETS!

PROPORTIONS

To give the characters a cute look, the head must be much larger than the body. The body should be small and short. If the body is measured as one unit, the head should be two and a half units.

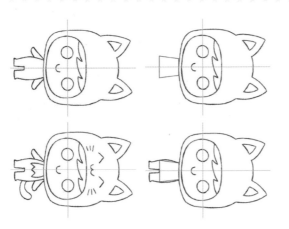

THE BODY

Extend the centre line of the face to the level of the feet. Starting with a simple shape, sketch the body and add other elements like arms, legs and tail.

THE HEAD

Start by drawing a simple geometric shape, such as a circle in this example, then trace the axis of the eyes and the centre line of the face. These will serve as landmarks to place the eyes, the mouth and the rest of the elements of the face.

HANDS AND FEET

Hands and feet are very simple and without real fingers. If you wish, you can detail them a little more while keeping them rounded with simple proportions.

hands

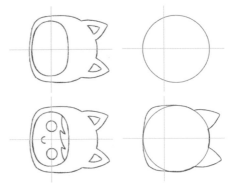

feet

OUTLINES

The outlines are often thick. To draw them, use a permanent felt tip pen that does not smudge when colouring. You can use finer felt tip pens on other elements to create contrast or to mark certain details. In this example, the cat's face and the character's mouth are thinner than the other outlines.

shadows

ADDING COLOUR

In kawaii we usually use solid colors, but you can add some simple shadows to give depth to the characters without worrying about realism. Use different marker colours to fill the solid areas and similar but darker shades to add the shadows.

In this book, you will find a huge range of drawings! To help you navigate, you'll find a symbol at the top of each page to indicate the theme.

🐾 Animals ❌ Food 🚗 Transport

🍃 Plants ⬅️ Household Objects 🌐 Around the World

🐚 Characters

FACIAL EXPRESSIONS

The expressions are simplified and are distinguished by the absence of a nose. There are so many variations that will give personality to your characters! Which one do you like best?

Bee

☆ ☆

☆ Beehive ☆

Caterpillar

☆ Butterfly ☆

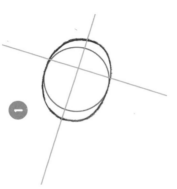

Spider ☆

1

5

2

6

3

7

4

8

☆ Ladybird ☆

☆ Snail ☆

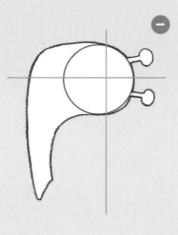

1

2

3

4

5

6

☆ Shell ☆

4

8

3

7

2

6

1

5

Crab ☆

☆ Tortoise ☆

☆ **Puffer Fish** ☆

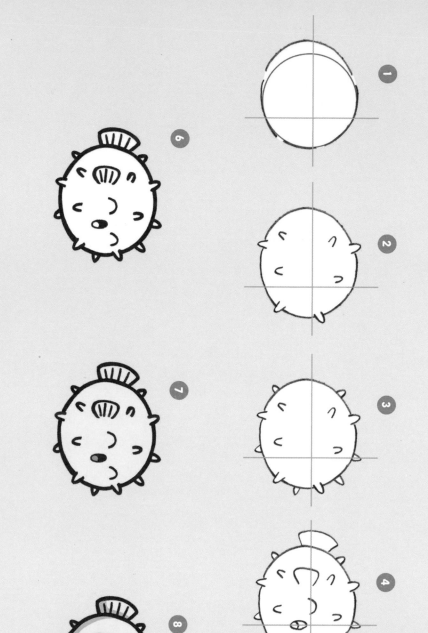

☆ Goldfish ☆

4

8

3

7

2

6

1

5

Squid

☆ Octopus ☆

☆ Jellyfish ☆

Seahorse

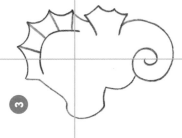

Whale

☆ Ray ☆

☆ Shark ☆

Orca

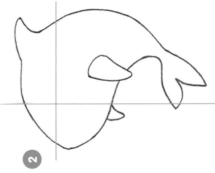

Dolphin ☆ ☆

☆ Seal ☆

Penguin

Flamingo ☆ ☆

Ostrich

☆ Peacock ☆

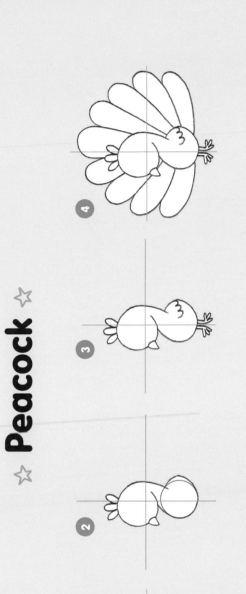

☆ Pigeon ☆

Swan ☆

Owl

4

8

☆ Parrot ☆

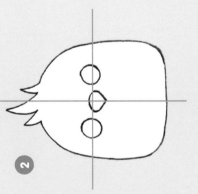

3

7

2

6

1

5

Feather

☆ Robin ☆

1

2

3

4

5

6

7

Chick

☆ Mouse ☆

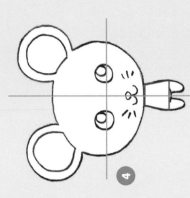

2

4

3

8

1

6

5

7

☆ **Hamster** ☆

1

2

3

4

5

6

7

Rabbit

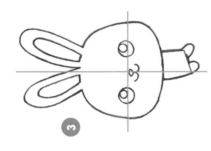

Ginger Cat

☆ Black Cat ☆

1

2

3

4

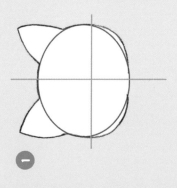

5

6

7

☆ Grey Cat ☆

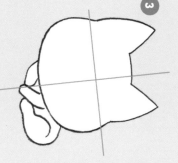

Poodle

Dog

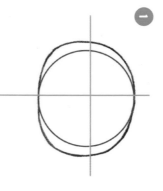

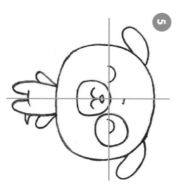

☆ Sheep ☆

3

7

2

6

1

5

4

8

46

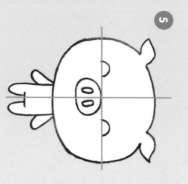

Pig

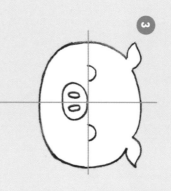

Cow ☆

☆

8

7

6

5

4

3

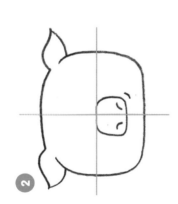

2

1

Elephant ☆ ☆

1

2

3

4

5

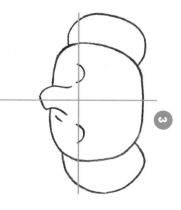

6

7

8

☆ Hippopotamus ☆

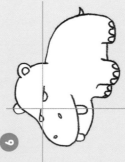

Giraffe

☆ Lion ☆

3

4

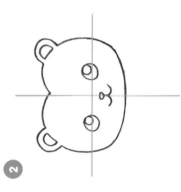

7

8

2

6

1

5

Camel

☆ ☆

1

2

3

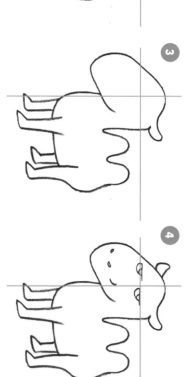

4

5

6

7

☆ Zebra ☆

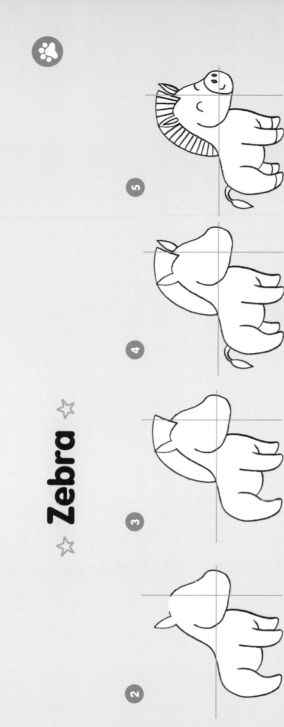

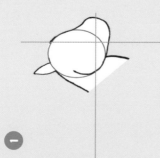

☆ Unicorn ☆

1

2

3

4

5

6

7

8

9

Dragon ☆ ☆

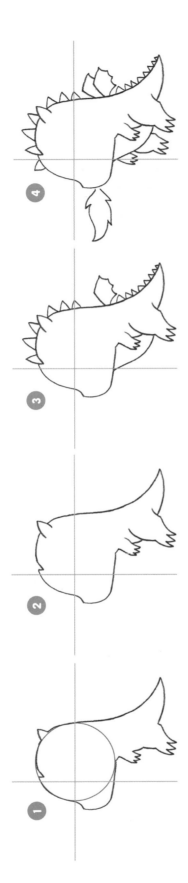

Dinosaur

☆ Snake ☆

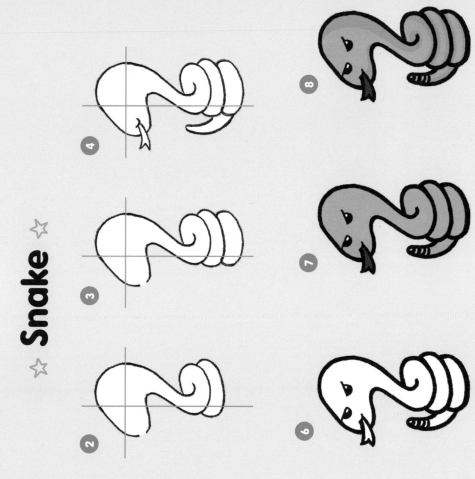

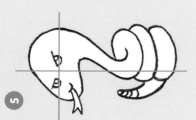

Gorilla

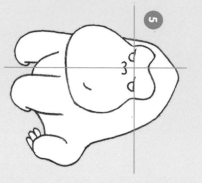

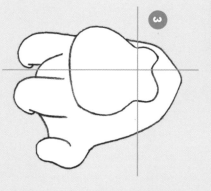

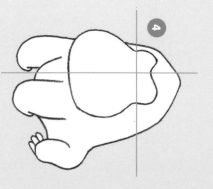

☆ Monkey ☆

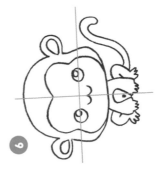

Llama

☆ Koala ☆

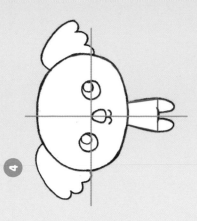

1

2

3

4

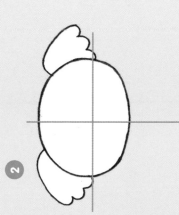

5

6

7

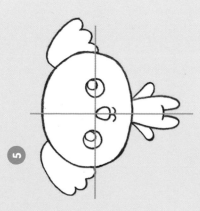

8

Red Panda

1

2

3

4

5

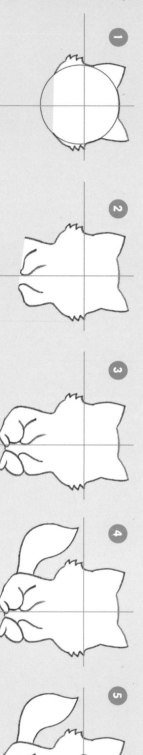

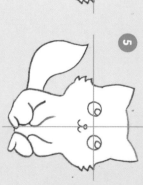

6

7

8

9

☆ Panda ☆

1

2

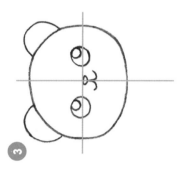

3

4

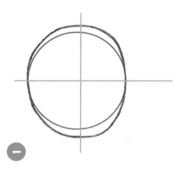

5

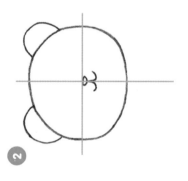

6

7

8

Polar Bear

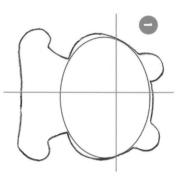

1

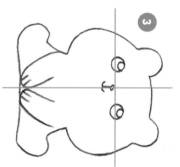

2

3

4

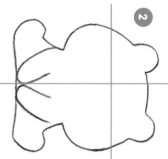

5

6

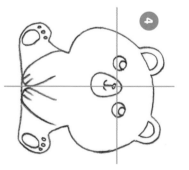

7

☆ Skunk ☆

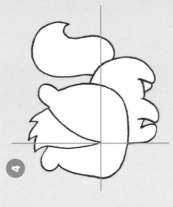

2

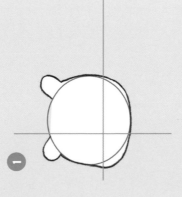

1

3

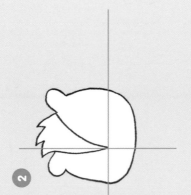

4

6

5

8

7

{}

Beaver

1

2

3

4

5

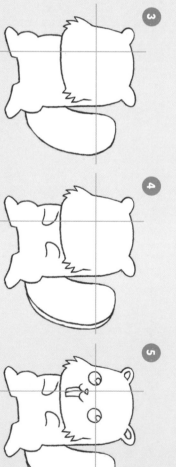

6

7

8

9

Fox

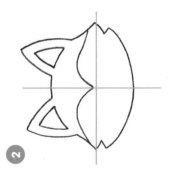

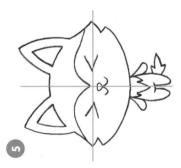

67

☆ **Doe** ☆

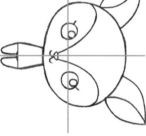

 Reindeer ☆

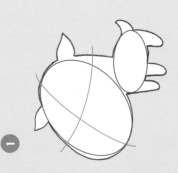

☆ Wolf ☆

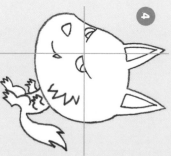

Bat

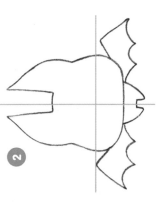

Squirrel

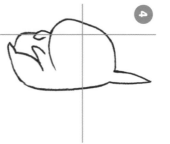

☆ Hedgehog ☆

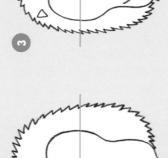

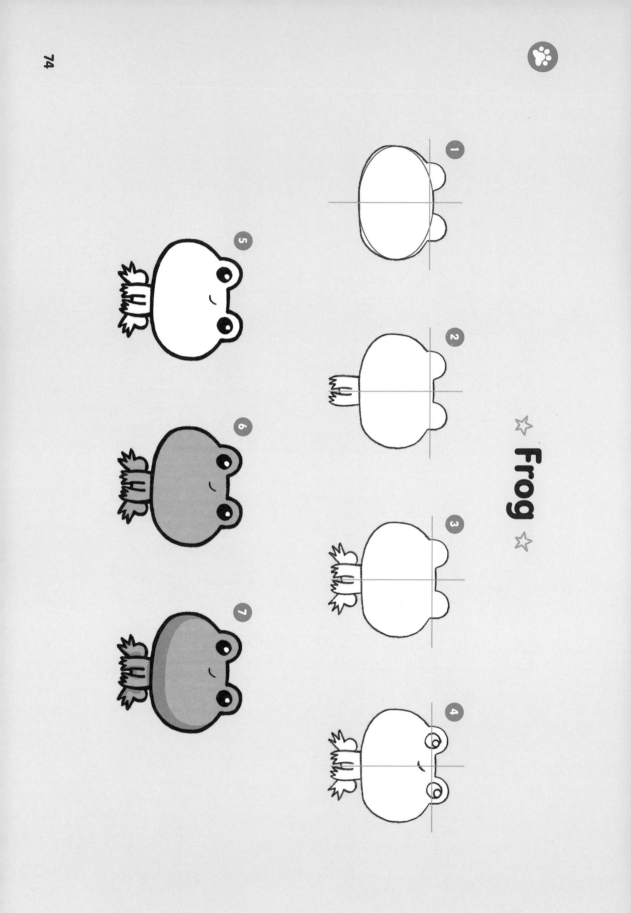

Frog

☆ Lily Pad and Flower ☆

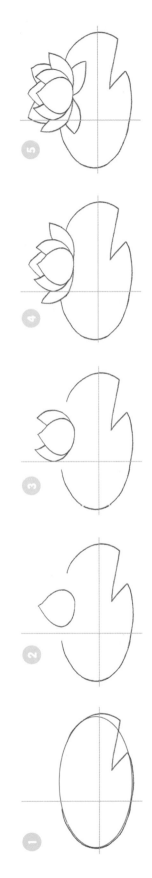

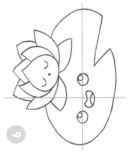

Rose

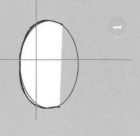

1

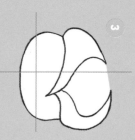

2

3

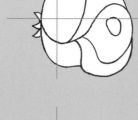

4

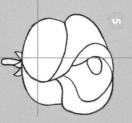

5

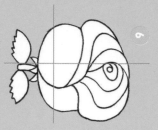

6

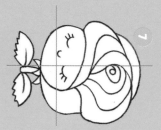

7

8

9

10

☆ Tulip ☆

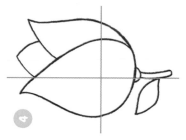

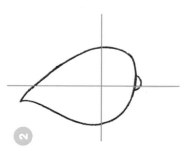

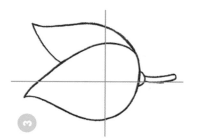

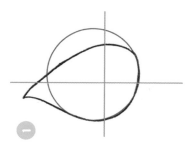

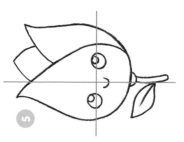

☆ Sunflower ☆

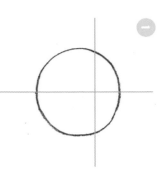

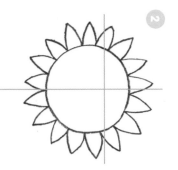

Daisy

5

4

3

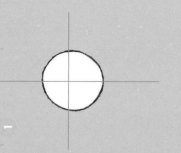

2

1

9

8

7

6

Little Cactus

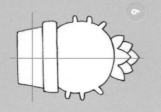

1

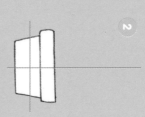

2

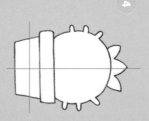

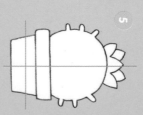

☆ Big Cactus ☆

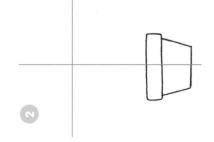

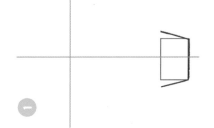

☆ Aloe Vera ☆

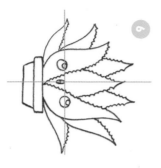

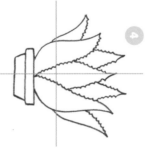

Bonsaï

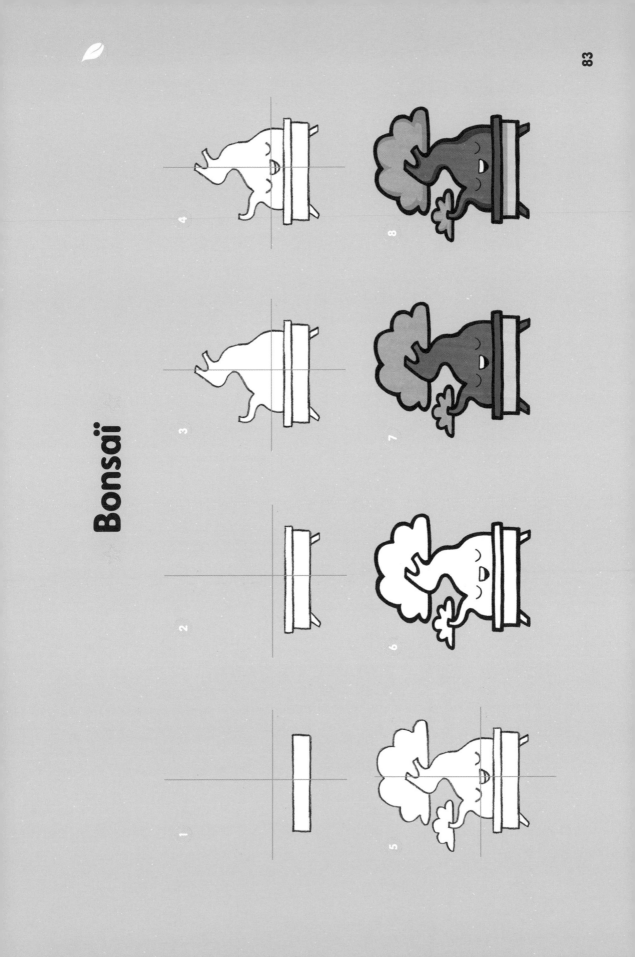

84

Shamrock

1

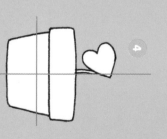

2

3

4

5

6

7

8

9

☆ Dandelion ☆

4

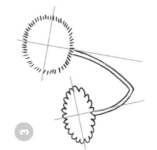

3

2

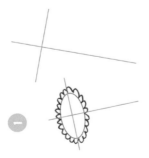

1

8

7

6

5

Lily of the Valley ☆

1

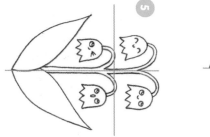

2

3

4

5

6

7

8

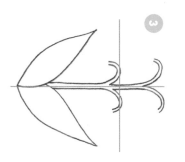

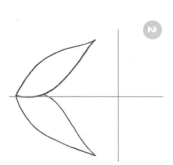

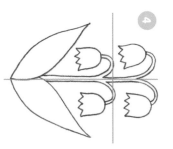

Holly

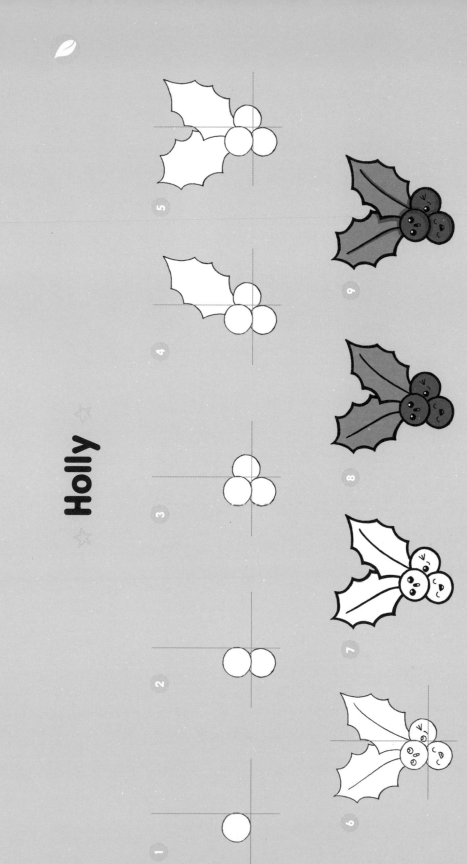

Log

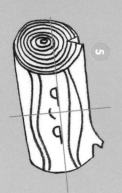

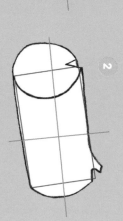

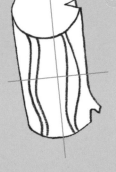

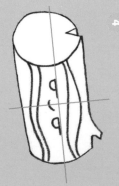

☆ Leaf ☆

Acorn ☆

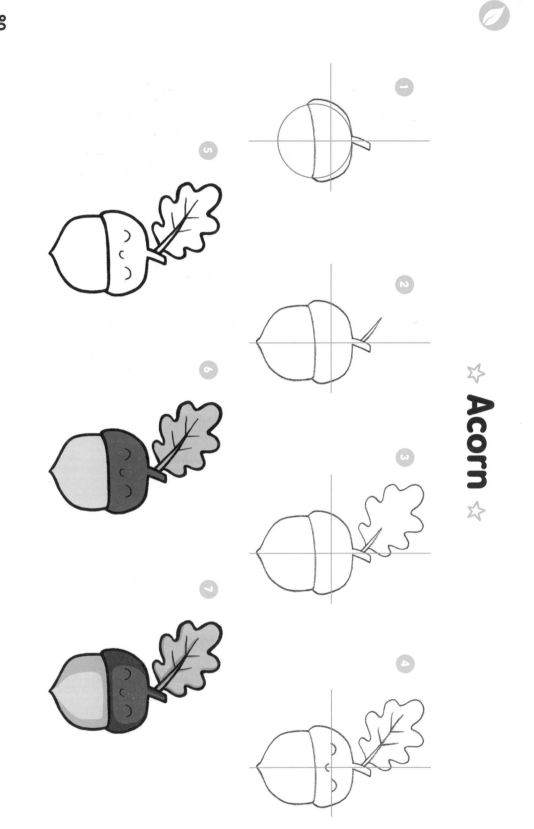

Mushroom

1
2
3
4
5
6
7

91

Garlic

Onion

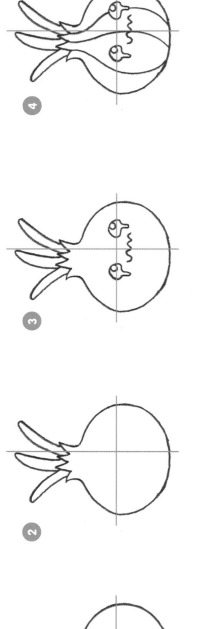

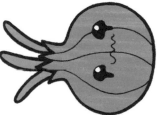

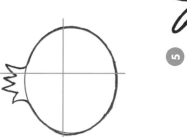

Chili

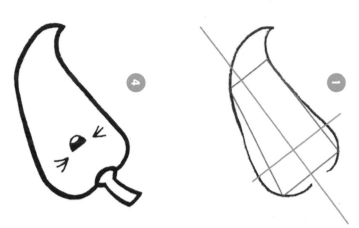

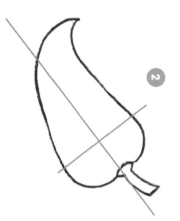

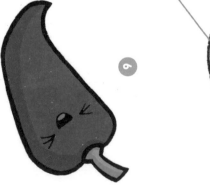

☆ Corn on the Cob ☆

4

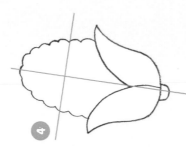

3

2

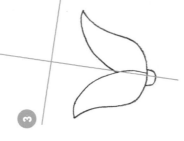

8

7

6

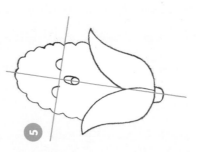

5

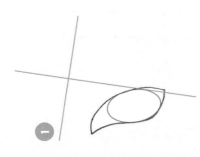

1

4

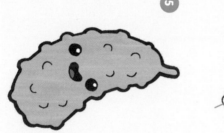

1

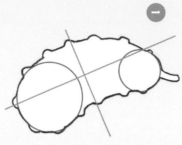

5

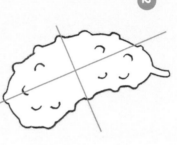

2

☆ Pickle ☆

6

3

Radish

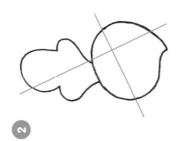

3

6

2

5

1

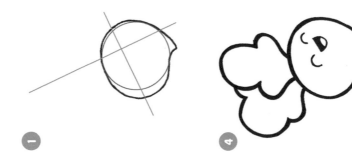

4

Beetroot

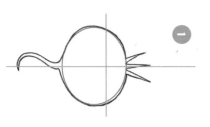

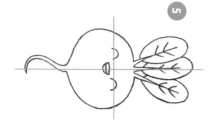

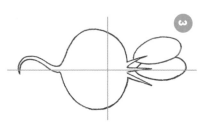

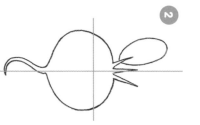

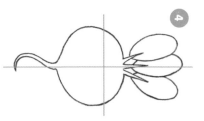

☆ Lettuce ☆

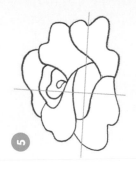

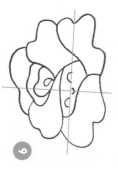

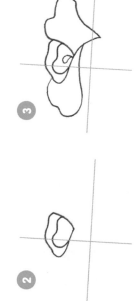

☆ Cauliflower ☆

1

2

3

4

5

6

7

8

9

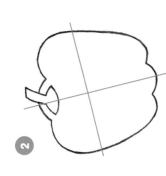

3

6

Bell Pepper

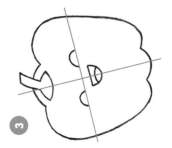

2

5

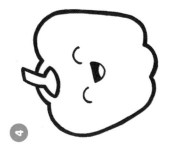

1

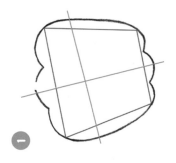

4

Broccoli

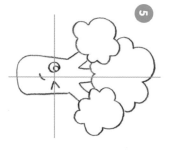

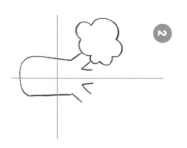

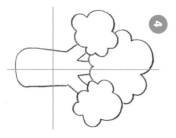

☆ **Leek** ☆

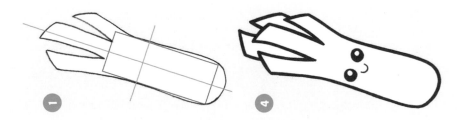

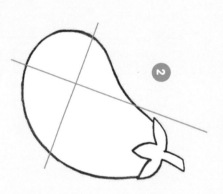

1

2

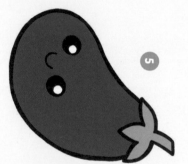

3

4

5

6

☆ **Aubergine** ☆

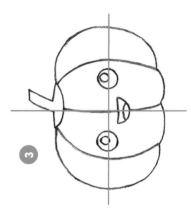

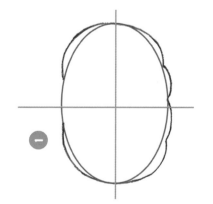

Pumpkin

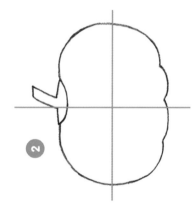

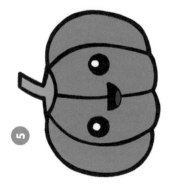

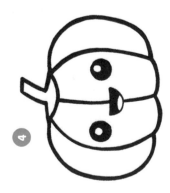

Carrot

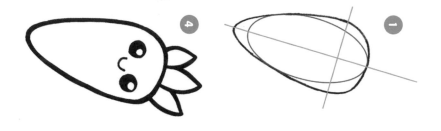

☆ Pea Pod ☆

4

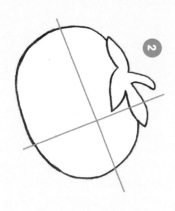

1

☆ **Tomato** ☆

2

5

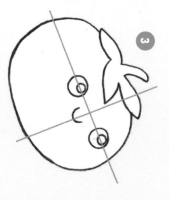

6

3

Ravioli

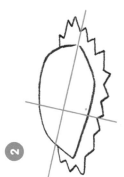

1

2

3

4

5

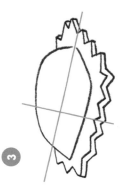

6

7

Swiss Cheese

1

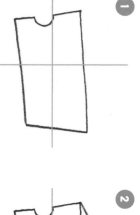

2

3

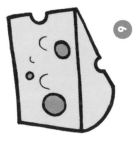

4

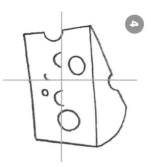

5

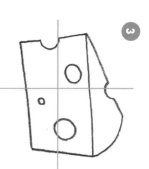

6

7

☆ Camembert ☆

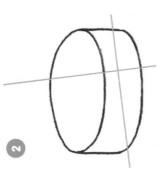

4

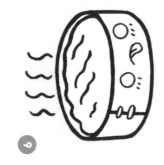

7

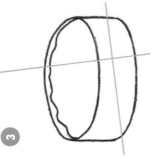

6

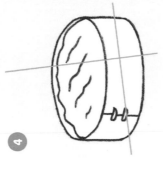

2

1

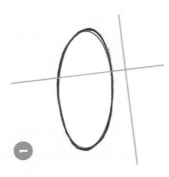

8

5

☆ Sandwich ☆

1

2

3

4

5

6

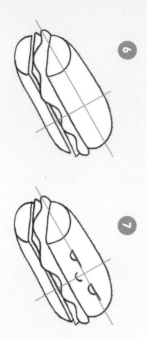

7

8

9

10

Baguette

3

6

9

2

5

8

1

4

7

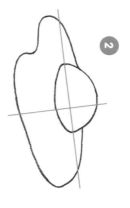

Fried Egg

☆ Boiled Egg ☆

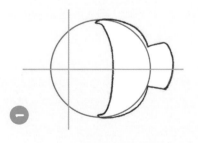

Chicken Leg

Steak

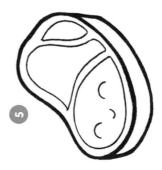

Hot Dog

1

5

2

6

3

7

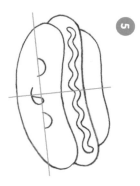

4

8

☆ Pizza ☆

Hamburger

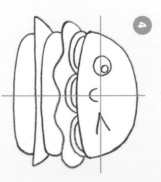

Fries

1

3

2

5

6

4

Salt and Pepper

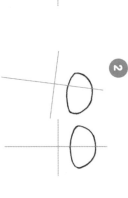

☆ Soup ☆

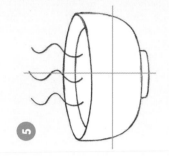

1

2

3

4

5

6

7

8

9

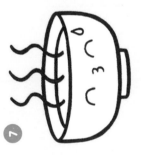

124

Onigiri

Sushi

1

2

3

4

5

6

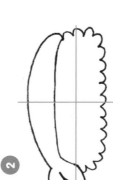

7

5

1

6

2

7

3

8

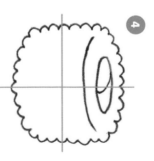

4

California Roll

126

☆ Maki ☆

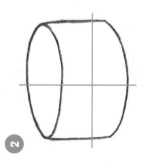

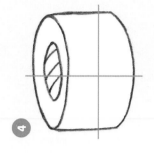

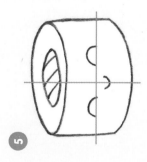

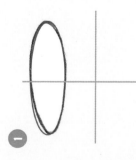

☆ Teabag ☆

1

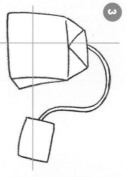

2

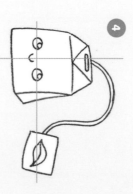

3

4

5

6

7

Cup of Tea

Teapot

☆ Hot Chocolate ☆

☆ Milk Carton ☆

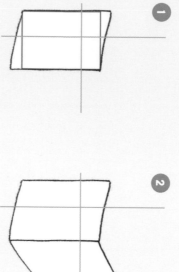

1

2

3

4

5

6

7

8

9

3

6

Glass of Milk

2

5

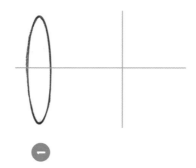

1

4

Baby Bottle

1

2

3

4

5

6

7

8

☆ Ice Cube ☆

☆ Soda Cup ☆

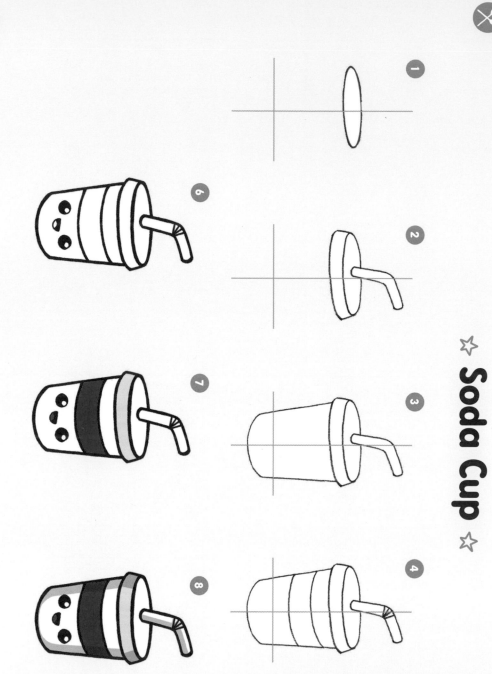

Soda Can

Cocktail

☆ Juice Carton ☆

1

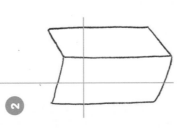

2

3

4

5

6

7

8

9

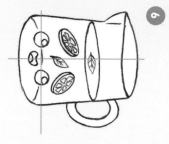

☆ Pitcher ☆

Clementine

4

3

2

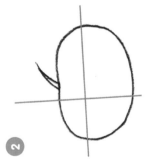

1

7

6

5

Lemon

☆ Avocado ☆

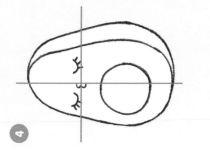

5

1

7

4

6

3

2

144

Grapefruit

Pineapple

Watermelon

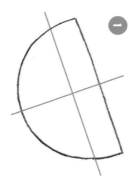

1

2

3

4

5

6

7

8

☆ Banana ☆

4

1

5

2

☆ Apple ☆

6

3

Pear

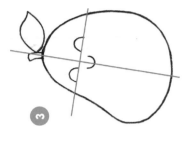

Cherries

1

2

3

4

5

6

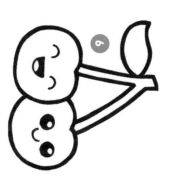

7

8

Raspberry ☆

3

2

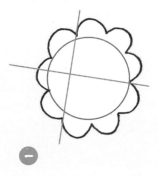

1

6

5

4

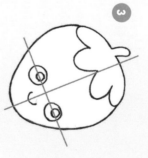

☆ **Strawberry** ☆

Yoghurt

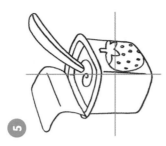

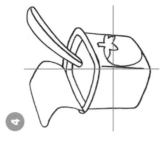

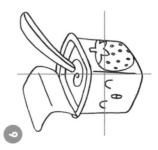

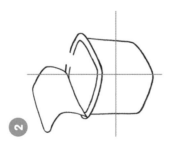

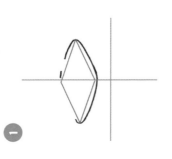

Jam Jar

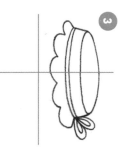

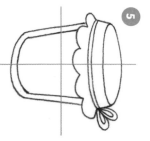

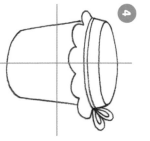

☆ Toast and Jam ☆

1

2

3

4

5

6

7

Chocolate Spread ☆

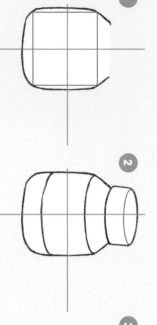

1

2

3

4

5

6

7

8

9

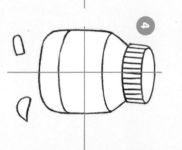

10

Chocolate Bar ☆

☆

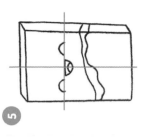

1

2

3

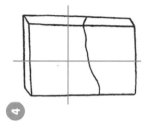

4

5

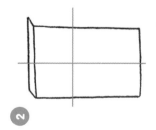

6

7

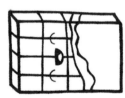

8

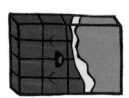

9

157

Muffin

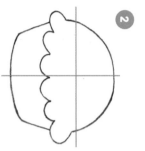

1

2

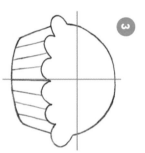

3

4

5

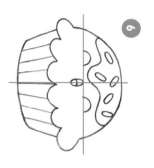

6

7

8

9

☆ Cupcake ☆

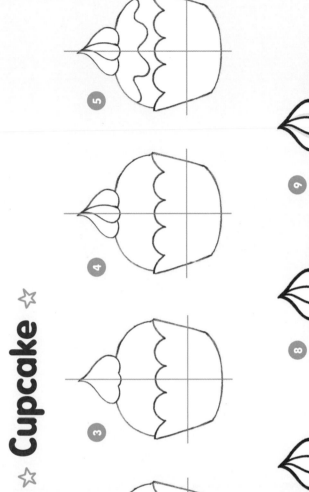

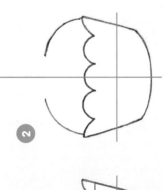

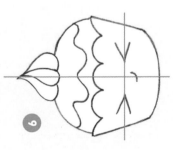

☆ Slice of Cake ☆

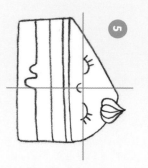

1

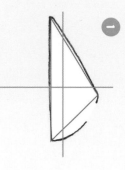

2

3

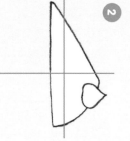

4

5

6

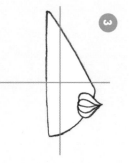

7

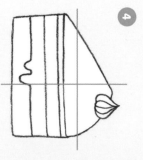

8

Rainbow Cake

1

2

3

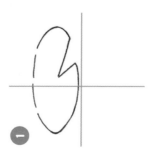

4

5

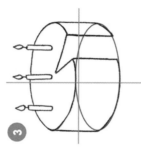

6

7

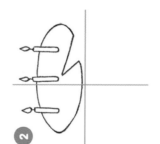

8

9

Christmas Pudding

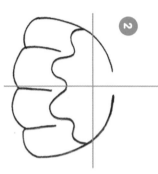

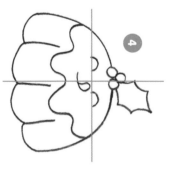

☆ Gingerbread Man ☆

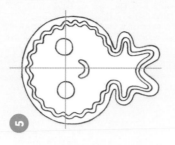

1

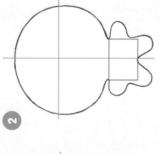

2

3

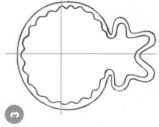

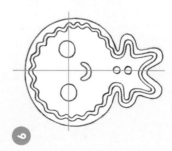

☆ Cookie ☆

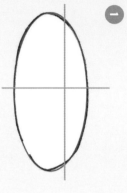

1

2

3

4

5

6

Pancakes

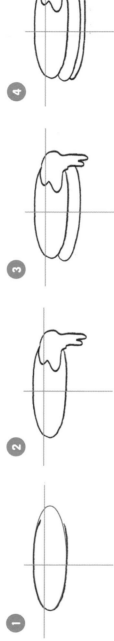

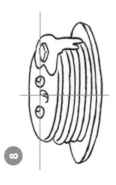

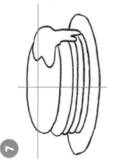

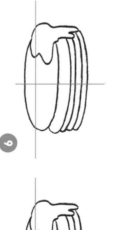

Croissant

1

2

3

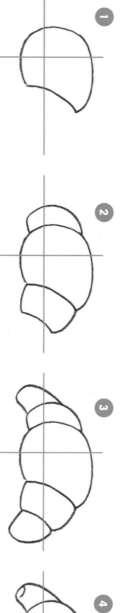

4

5

6

7

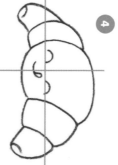

☆ Pain au Chocolat ☆

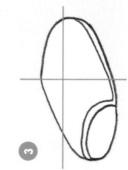

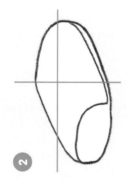

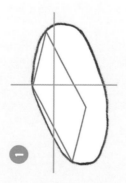

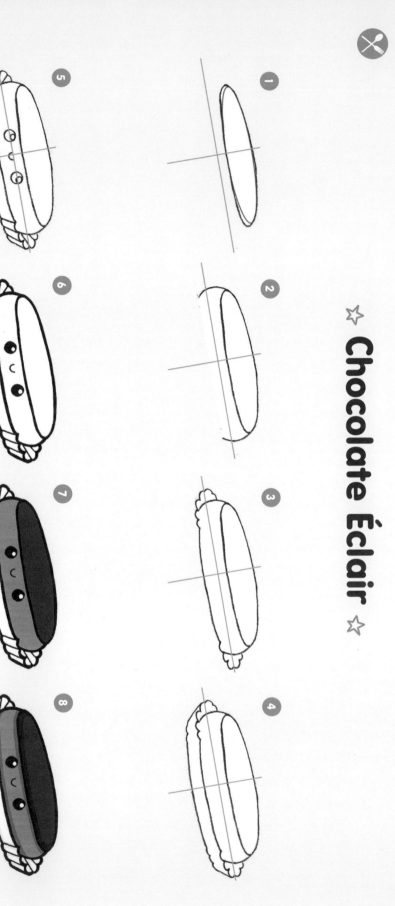

Chocolate Éclair

Chocolate Choux Bun

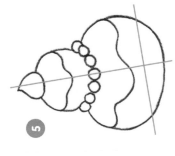

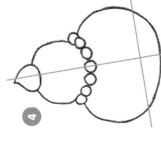

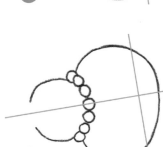

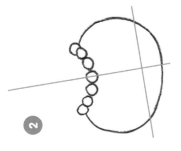

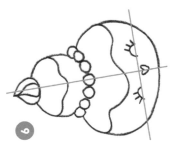

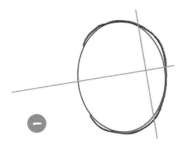

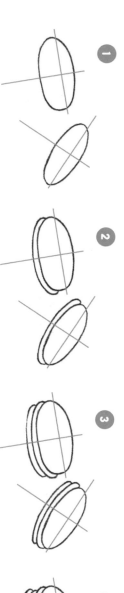

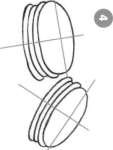

Macarons

1

2

3

4

5

6

7

8

9

☆ Donut ☆

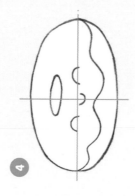

5

6

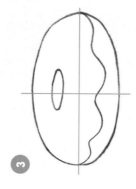

1

2

3

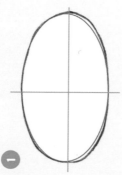

4

7

8

Candyfloss

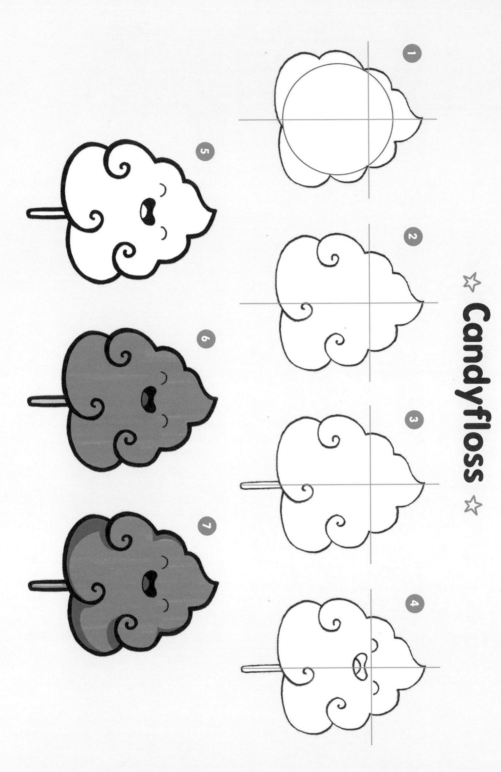

Toffee Apple

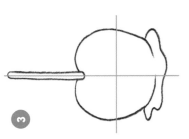

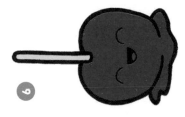

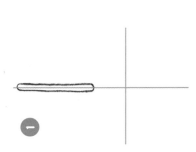

Popcorn

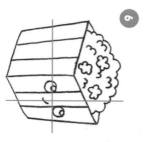

1

2

3

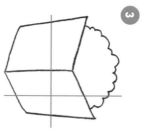

4

5

6

7

8

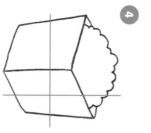

9

☆ Candy Cane ☆

4

1

2

3

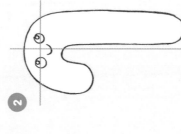

5

6

7

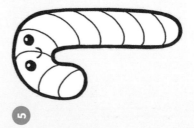

☆ Lollipop ☆

Sweet

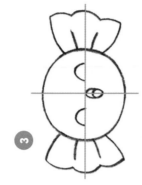

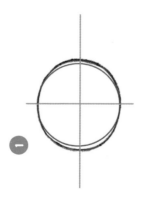

Easter Basket

1

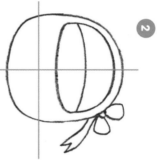

2

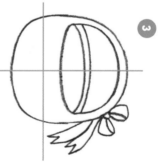

3

4

☆ Easter Egg ☆

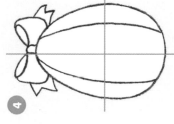

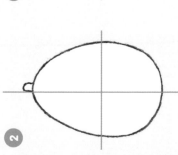

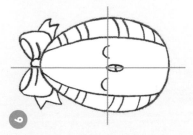

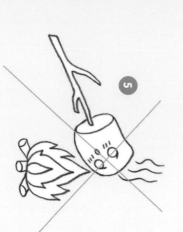

Marshmallow ☆

1

2

3

4

5

6

7

8

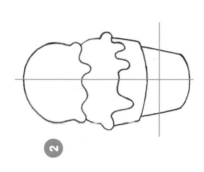

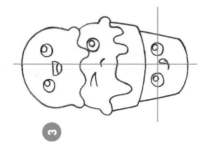

Ice Cream Cone

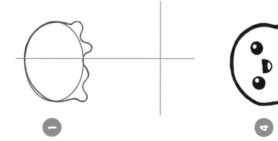

181

Sundae

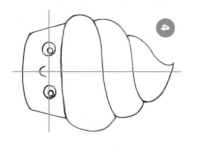

1

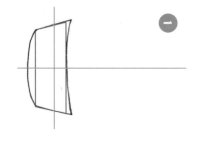

2

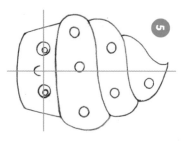

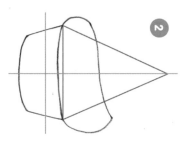

3

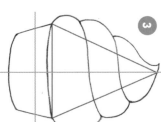

5

4

6

☆ Soft Ice Cream ☆

Ice Lolly

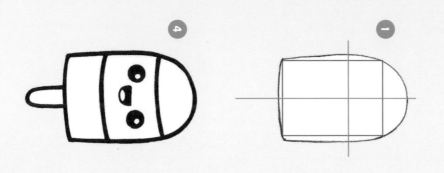

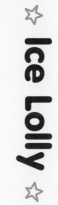

Choc Ice

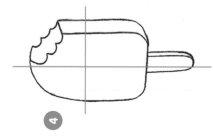

2

3

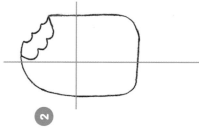

4

1

5

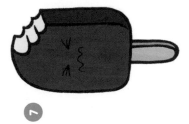

6

7

8

Fridge

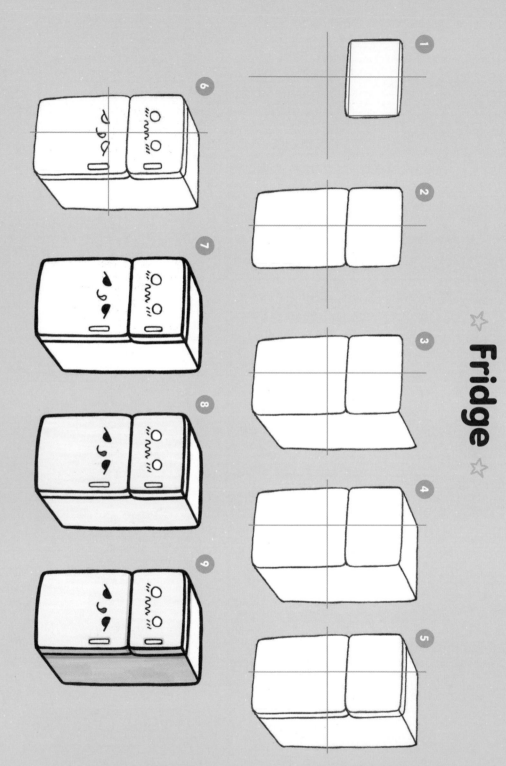

☆ Oven ☆

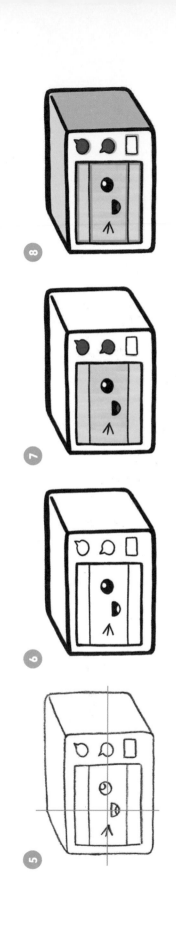

☆ Toaster ☆

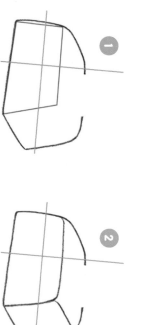

☆ Kettle ☆

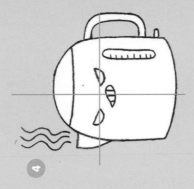

7

4

6

3

5

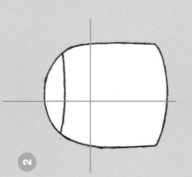

2

1

Casserole Dish

190

☆ Cauldron ☆

☆ Saucepan ☆

1

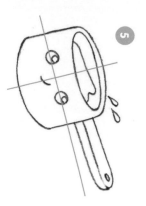

2

3

4

5

6

7

8

☆ Ladle ☆

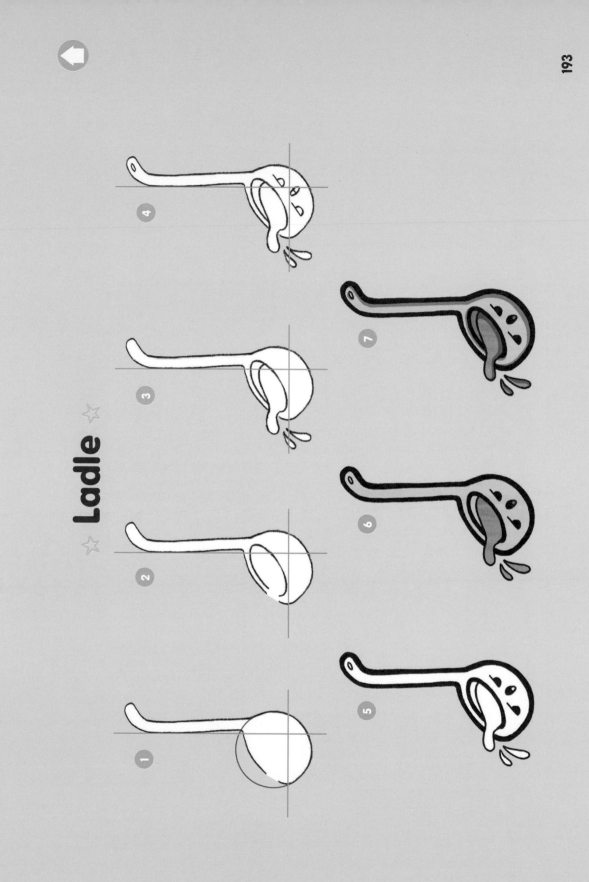

1

2

3

4

5

6

7

8

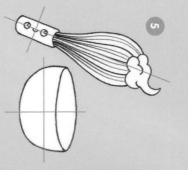

9

☆ Whisk and Bowl ☆

☆ Rolling Pin ☆

☆ **Knife** ☆

☆ Cutlery ☆

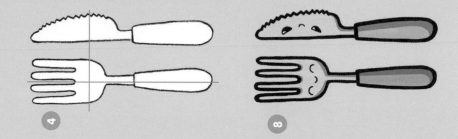

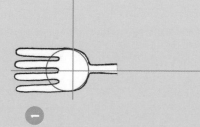

Grocery Bag

1

2

3

4

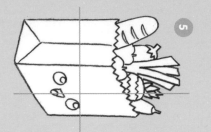

5

6

7

8

☆ Dustbin ☆

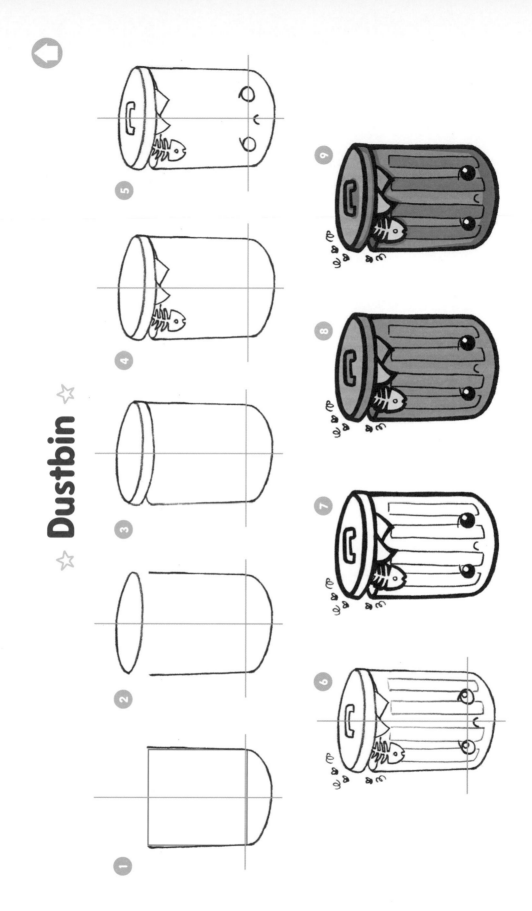

Flask ☆ ☆

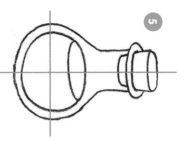

☆ Teeth ☆

1

2

3

4

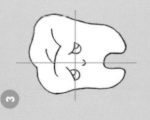

5

6

7

8

9

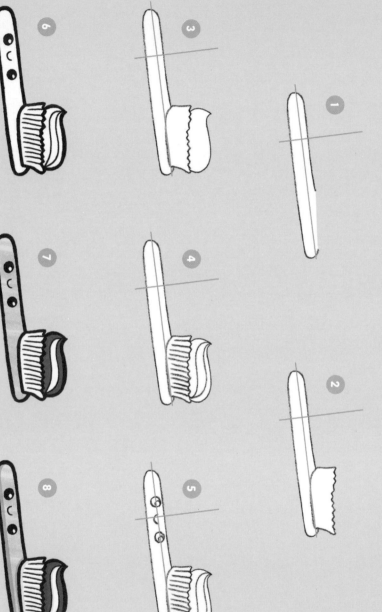

☆ **Toothbrush** ☆

☆ Toothpaste ☆

①

②

③

④

⑤

⑥

⑦

⑧

⑨

☆ **Plaster** ☆

1

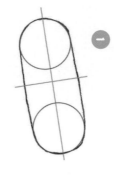

2

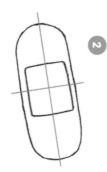

3

4

5

6

7

Thermometer ☆

Poop and Paper

☆ Tissues ☆

1

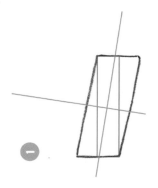

2

3

4

5

6

7

8

☆ Soap ☆

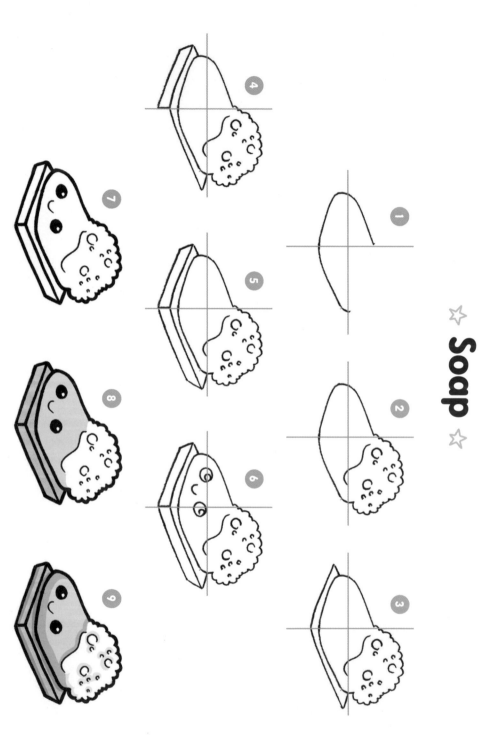

☆ Bathtub ☆

Perfume ☆

☆ Lipstick ☆

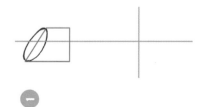

☆ **Nail Polish** ☆

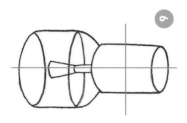

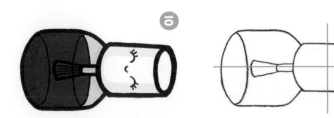

☆ Make-Up Palette ☆

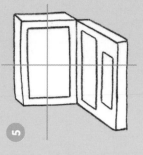

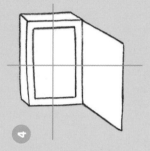

Hairbrush

Hairdryer ☆

☆

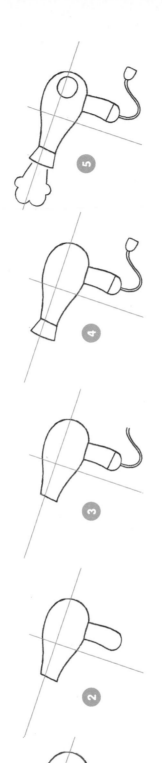

1

2

3

4

5

6

7

8

9

☆ Washing Machine ☆

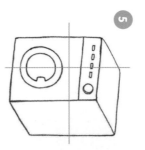

☆ Iron ☆

5

4

3

2

1

9

8

7

6

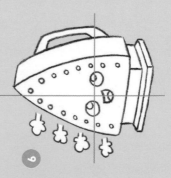

Vacuum Cleaner

1

2

3

4

5

6

7

8

9

10

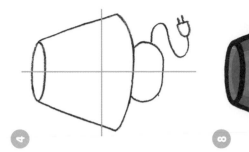

☆ Table Lamp ☆

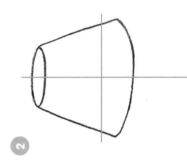

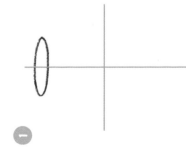

Alarm Clock ☆ ☆

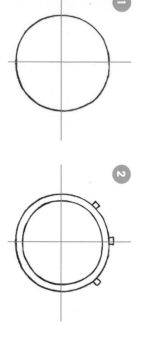

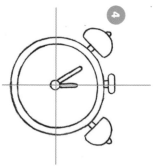

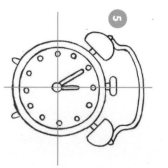

☆ Bed ☆

Armchair

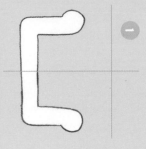

1

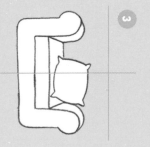

2

3

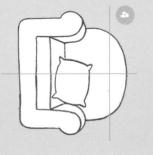

4

5

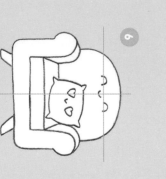

6

7

8

9

☆ Office Chair ☆

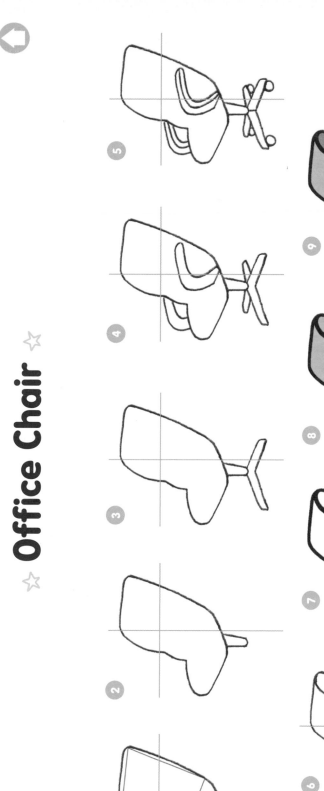

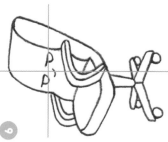

☆ Chair ☆

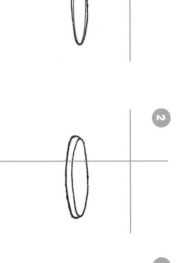

1

2

3

4

5

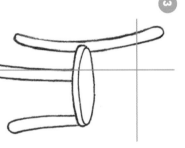

6

7

8

9

☆ Wardrobe ☆

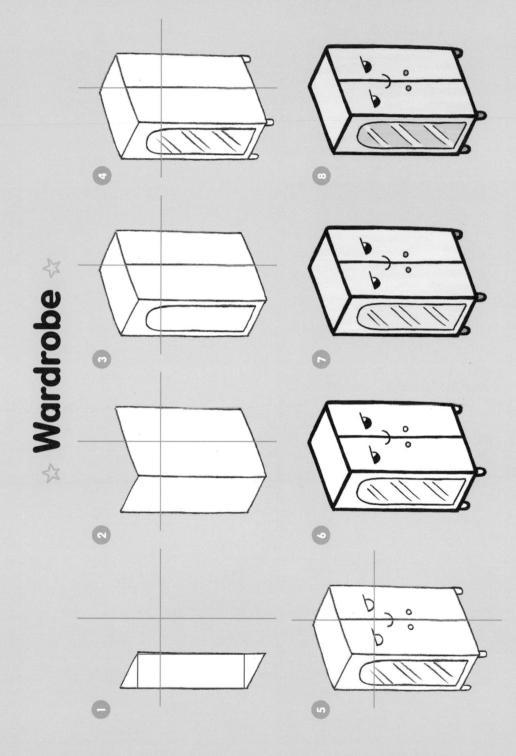

Treasure Chest

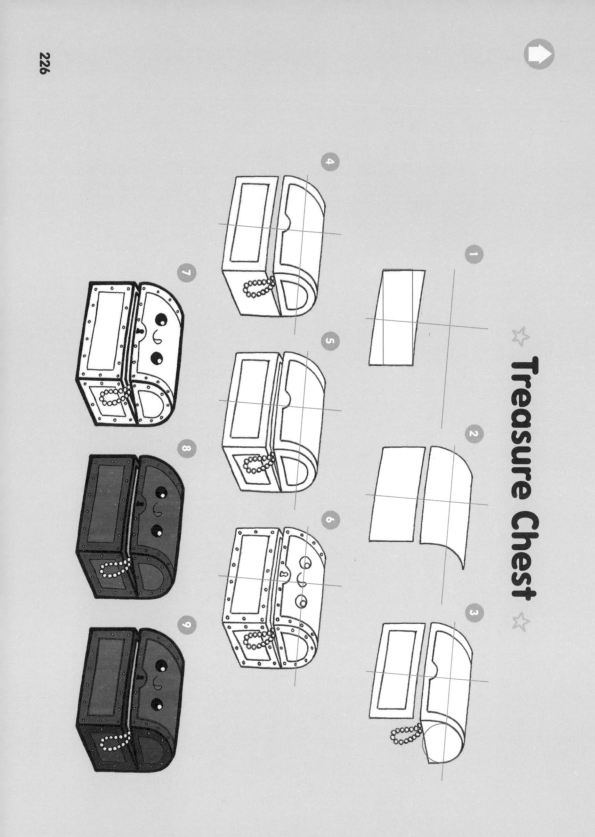

☆ Cardboard Box ☆

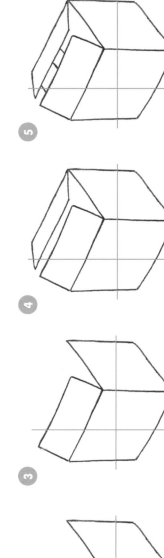

1

2

3

4

5

6

7

8

9

Bucket

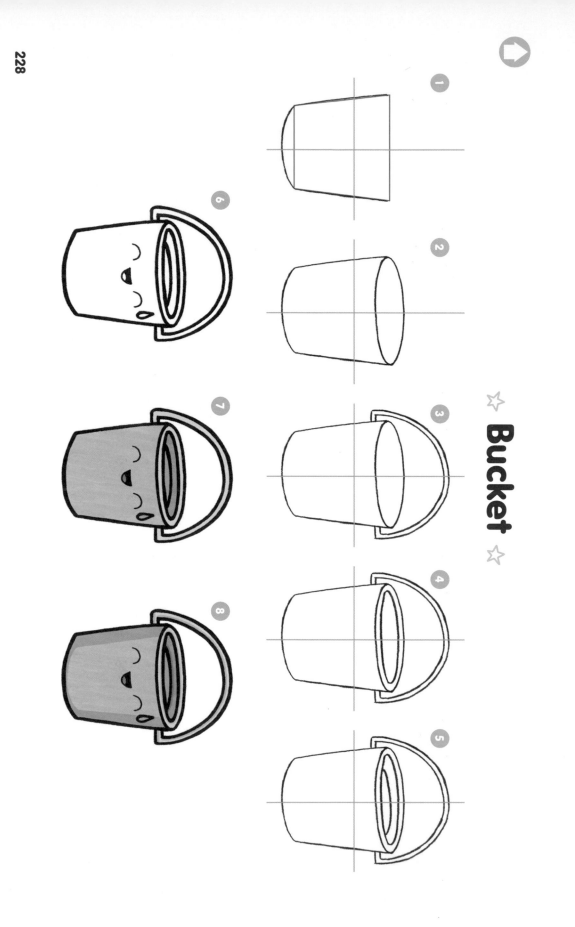

Watering Can

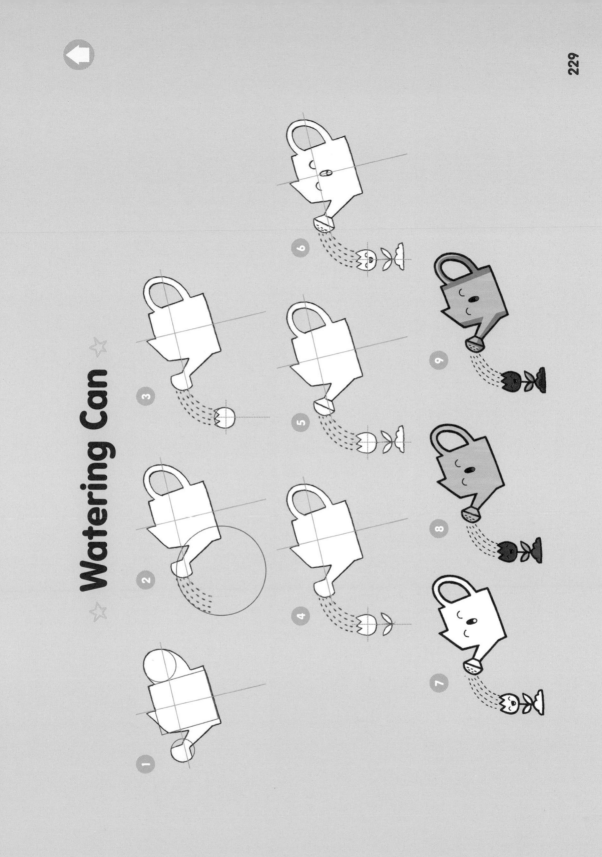

Gardening Tools

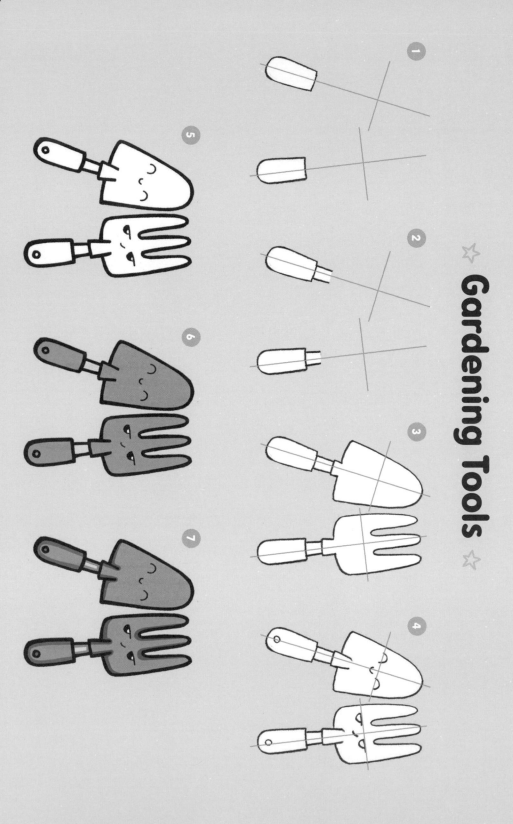

☆ Swiss Army Knife ☆

1

2

3

4

5

6

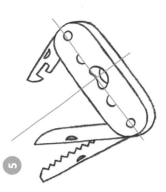

7

8

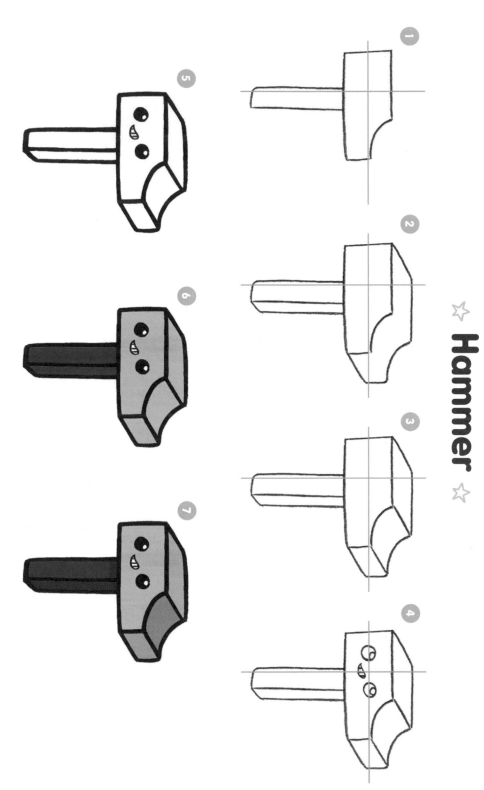

☆ **Hammer** ☆

1

2

3

4

5

6

7

Spanner

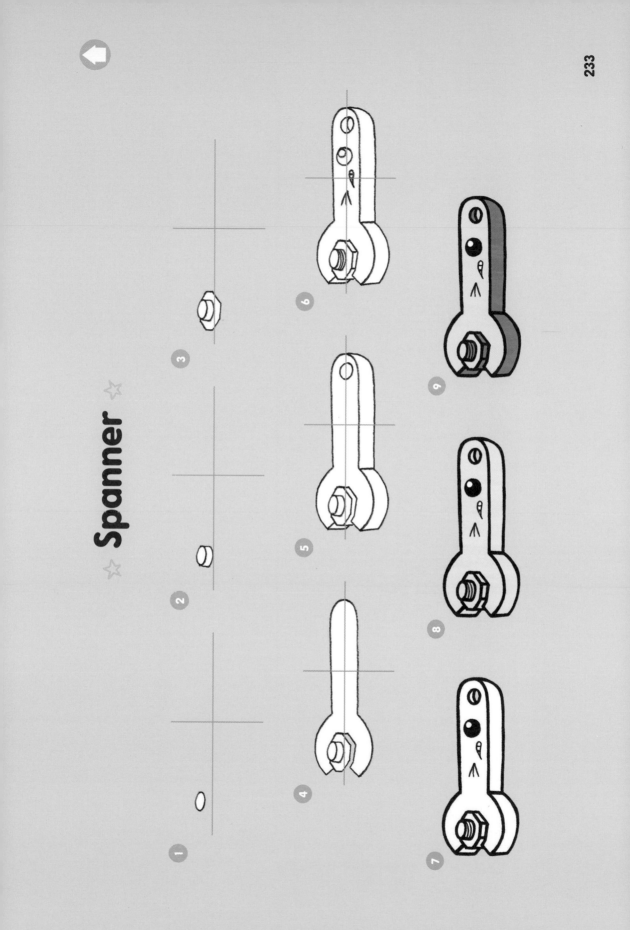

Screwdriver

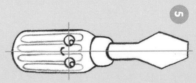

☆ Screw ☆

5

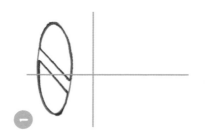

4

3

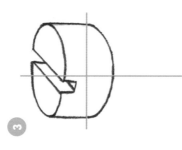

2

1

8

7

6

Paint Pot ☆

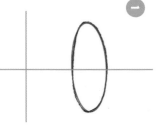

1

2

3

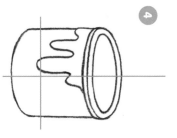

4

5

6

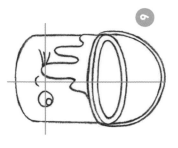

7

8

9

☆ Paint Palette ☆

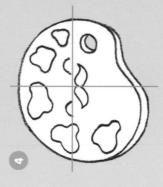

1

2

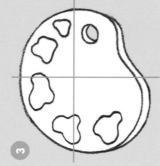

3

4

5

6

7

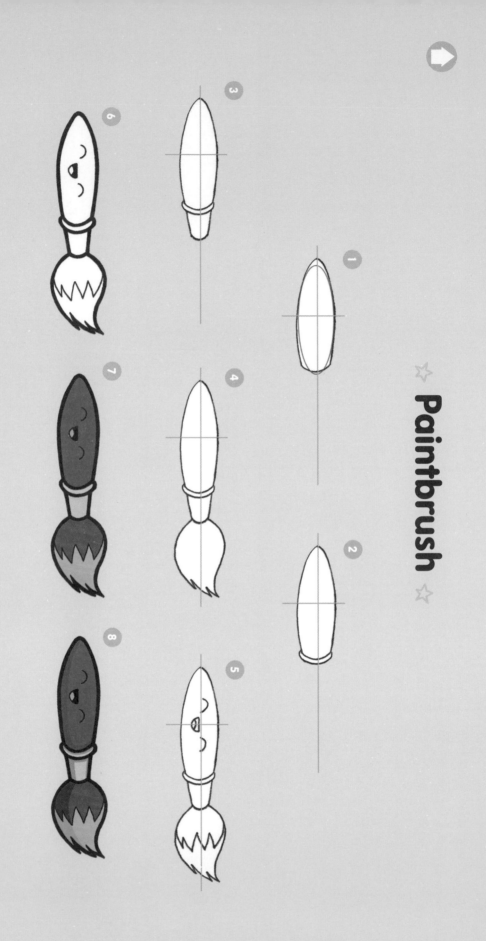

Paintbrush

☆ Pencil Crayon ☆

1

2

3

4

5

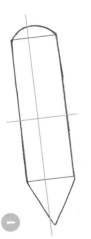

6

7

8

Pencil Sharpener ☆ ☆

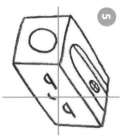

☆ Pencil Case ☆

1

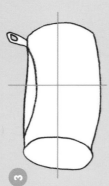

2

3

4

5

6

7

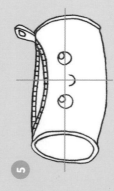

8

☆ Eraser ☆

☆ Scissors ☆

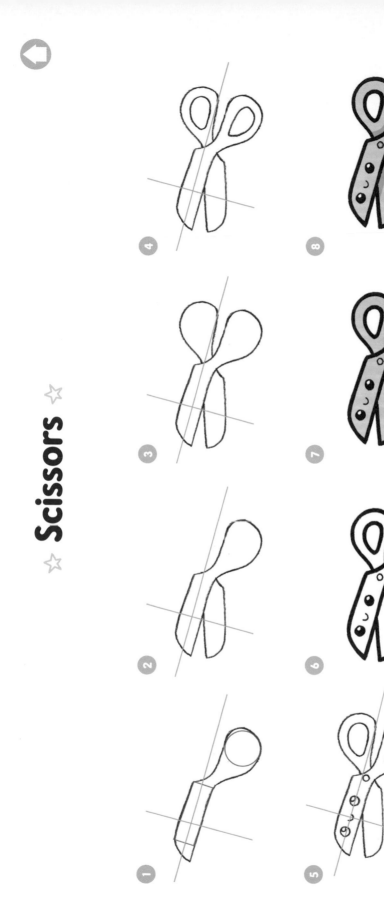

Sticky Tape ☆

5

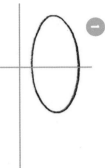

1

2

3

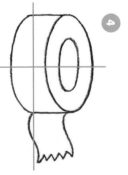

4

6

7

8

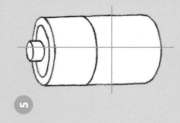

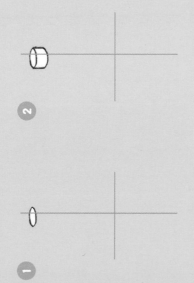

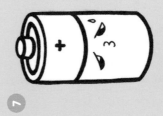

Battery ☆

☆

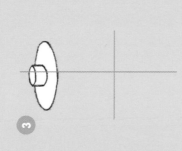

1

2

3

4

5

6

7

8

9

Torch ☆ ☆

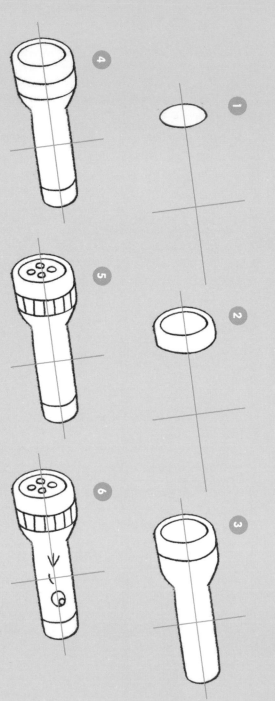

1

2

3

4

5

6

7

8

9

☆ Lightbulb ☆

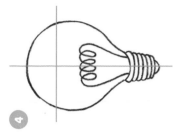

4

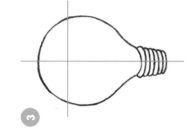

3

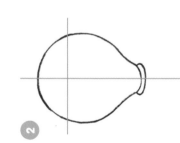

2

1

8

7

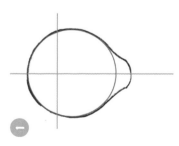

6

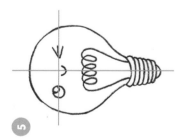

5

☆ **Match** ☆

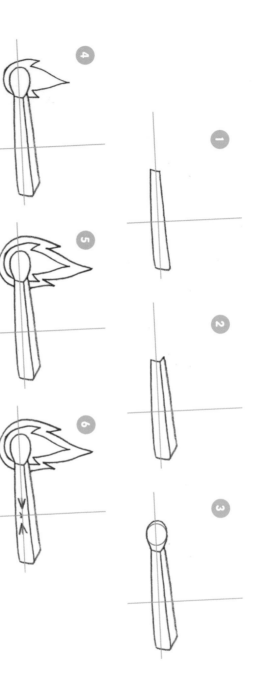

1

4

2

5

3

6

7

8

9

Candle

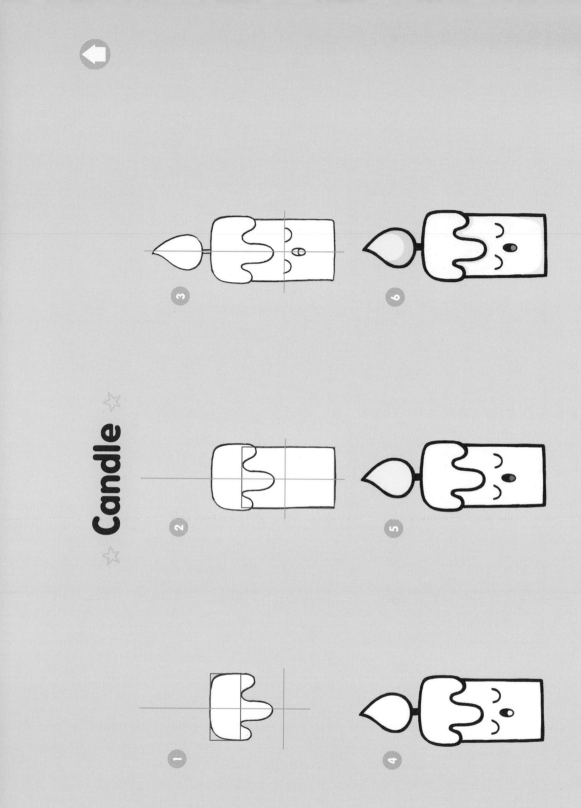

1

2

3

4

5

6

Snowglobe ☆ ☆

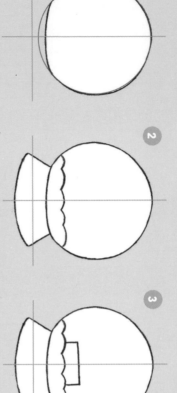

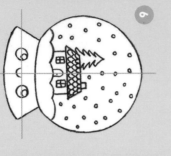

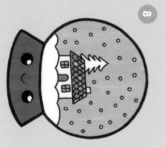

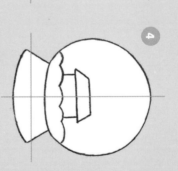

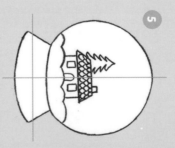

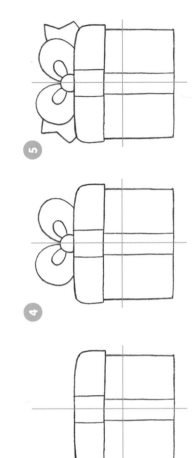

Gift ☆ ☆

1

2

3

4

5

6

7

8

9

☆ **Bauble** ☆

Christmas Tree

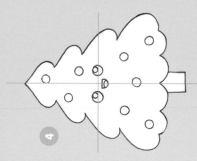

Bell ☆

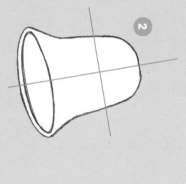

☆ Trumpet ☆

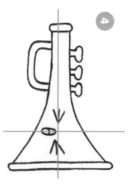

Accordion

1

3

2

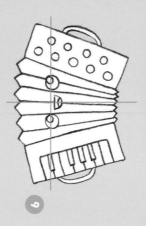

4

6

5

7

9

8

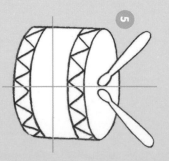

☆ **Drum** ☆

258

Maracas

1

☆ **Piano** ☆

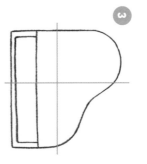

☆ Violin ☆

Electric Guitar

Acoustic Guitar

Saxophone

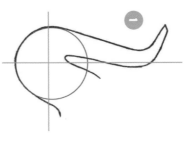

Harmonica

Musical Box ☆ ☆

1

2

3

4

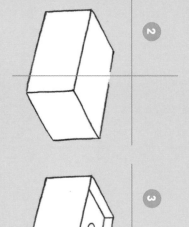

5

6

7

8

9

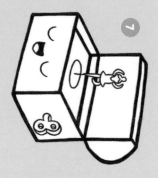

☆ Microphone ☆

5

4

3

2

1

10

9

8

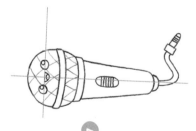

7

6

☆ USB Stick ☆

1

2

3

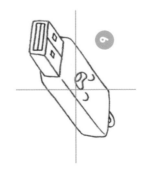

4

5

6

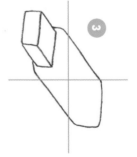

7

8

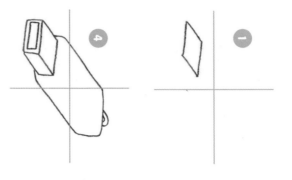

9

☆ Laptop ☆

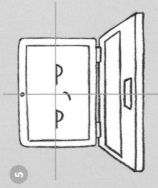

Smart Phone

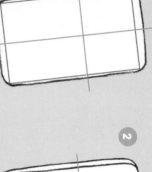

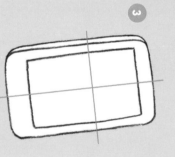

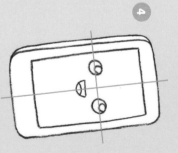

☆ Camera ☆

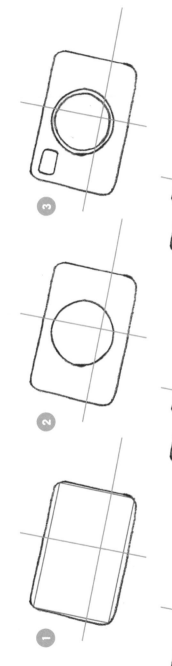

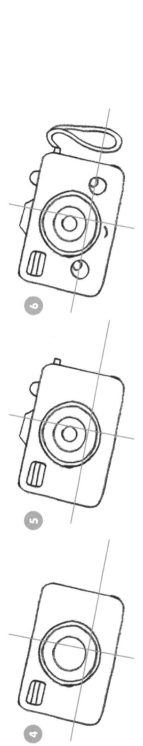

Basketball and Hoop

Bowling Ball and Skittle

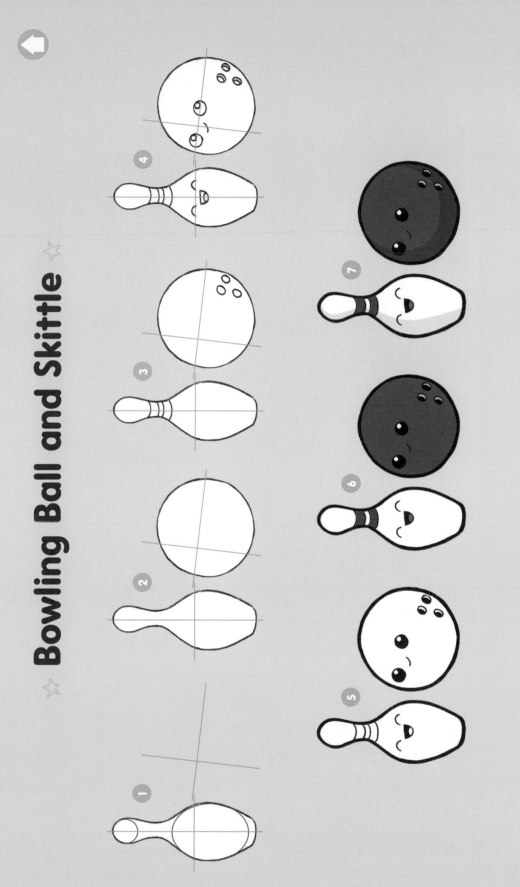

Ping Pong Ball and Paddle

☆ **Skateboard** ☆

☆ **Balloon** ☆

Crown

☆ ☆

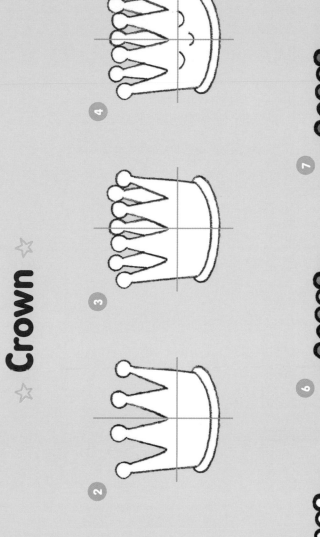

☆ Envelope ☆

1

2

3

4

5

6

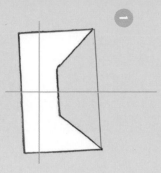

7

8

☆ Book ☆

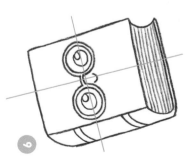

Key

Diamond ☆

1

2

3

4

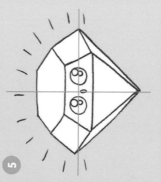

5

6

7

8

Calculator ☆ ☆

1

2

3

4

5

6

7

8

☆ Purse ☆

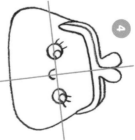

Backpack ☆

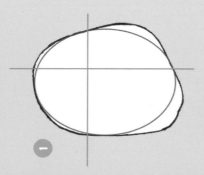

Suitcase ☆

5

6

7

8

2

1

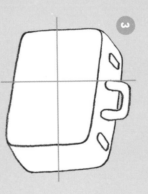

3

4

☆ Hat ☆

☆ **Cap** ☆

1

2

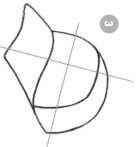

3

4

5

6

7

8

Flip-flops ☆

☆

4

3

2

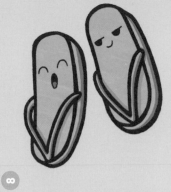

1

8

7

6

5

T-shirt

☆ Slippers ☆

1

2

3

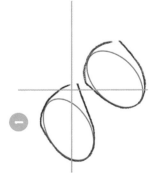

4

5

6

7

☆ **Fan** ☆

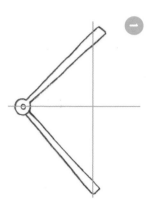

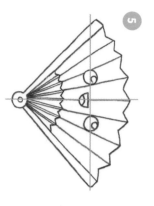

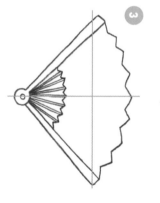

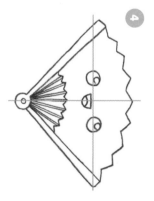

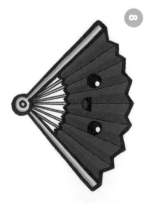

☆ Umbrella ☆

1

2

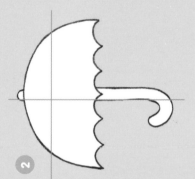

3

4

5

6

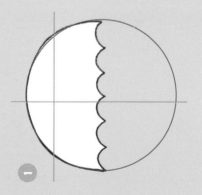

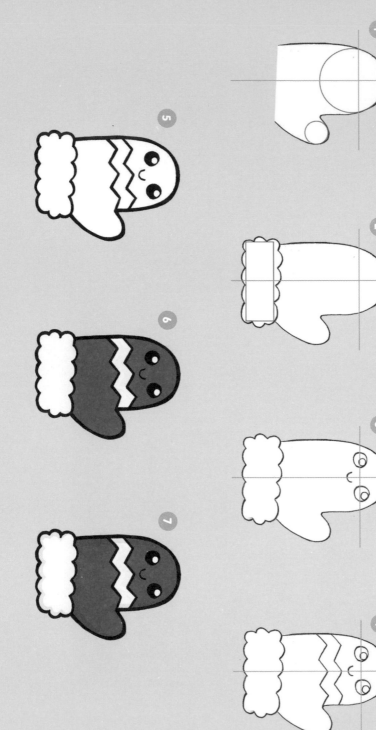

☆ Mitten ☆

Stocking ☆

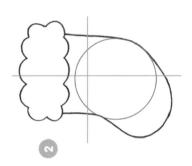

1

2

3

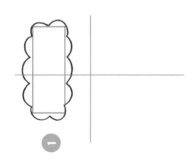

4

5

6

☆ **Father Christmas** ☆

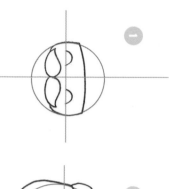

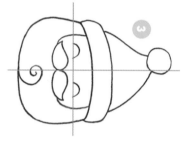

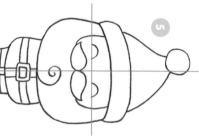

Mother Christmas

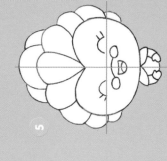

1

2

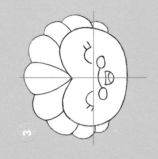

3

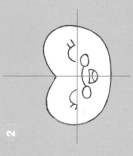

4

5

6

7

8

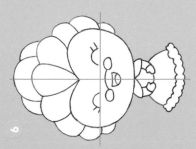

9

Snowman

1

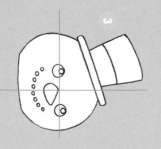

2

3

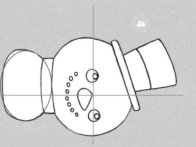

4

5

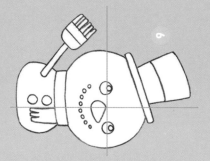

6

7

8

9

Elf ☆

☆

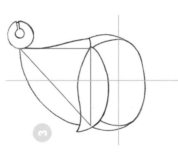

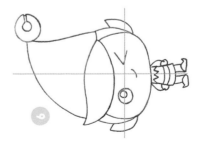

☆ Angel ☆

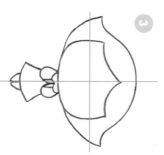

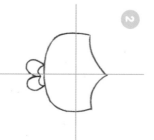

Devil

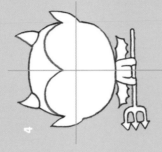

Skeleton

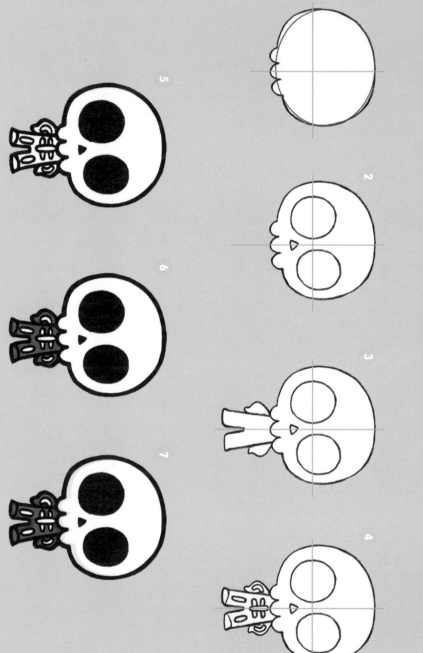

☆ Vampire ☆

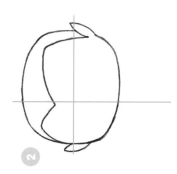

Witch ☆ ☆

Ghost

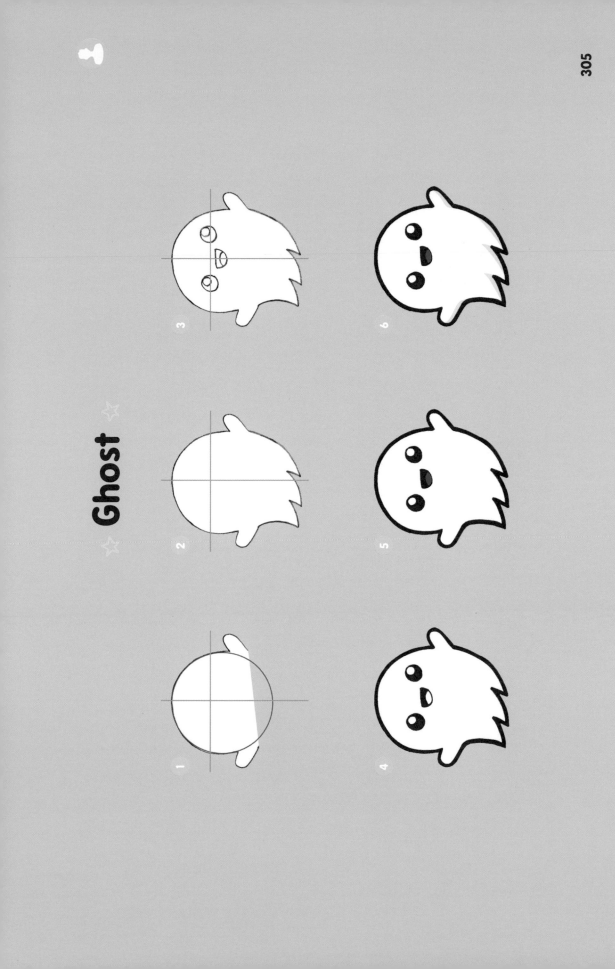

Voodoo Doll

☆ Scarecrow ☆

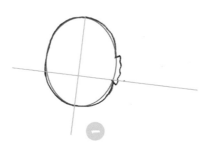

☆ **Knight** ☆

Princess

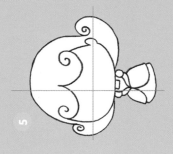

1

2

3

4

5

6

7

8

9

Pirate

1

2

3

4

5

 6

☆ Wizard ☆

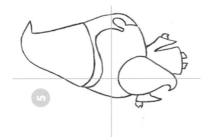

Mermaid ☆

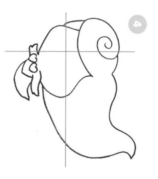

Fairy

Magic Lamp

☆ Genie ☆

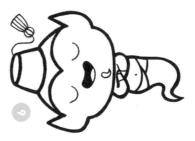

☆ **Explorer** ☆

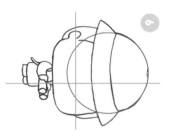

Mummy

1

2

3

4

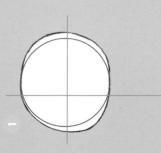

5

6

7

Pharaoh

1

2

3

4

5

6

7

8

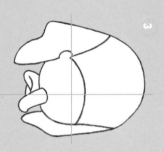

9

10

☆ Cleopatra ☆

☆ **Pink Kokeshi** ☆

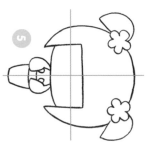

Blue Kokeshi

1

2

3

4

5

6

7

8

Green Kokeshi

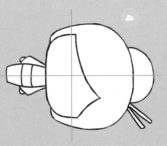

☆ Red Kokeshi ☆

☆ Goth Girl ☆

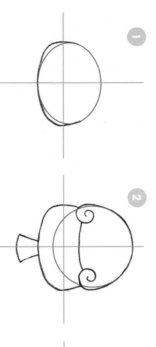

Rabbit Boy

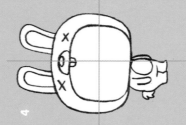

Little Red Riding Hood

☆ Ballerina ☆

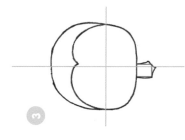

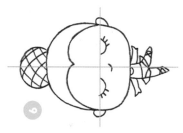

☆ **Chef** ☆

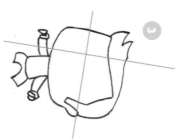

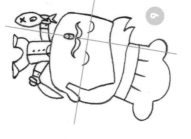

Astronaut

1

2

3

4

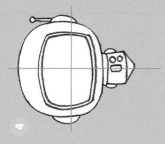

5

6

7

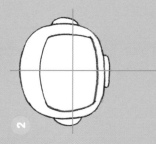

8

9

10

Alien

1

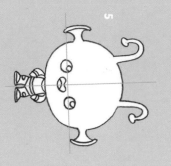

2

3

4

5

6

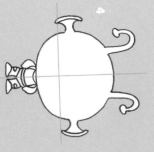

7

8

☆ Flying Saucer ☆

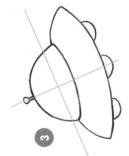

Rocket ☆ ☆

☆ Aeroplane ☆

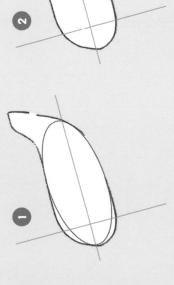

☆ Hot Air Balloon ☆

Helicopter ☆

☆

2

3

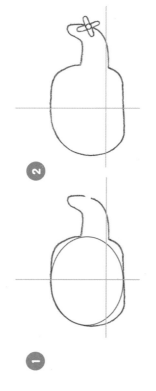

1

4

5

6

7

8

Fire Engine ☆

☆

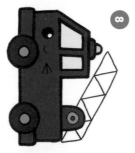

☆ Car ☆

1

2

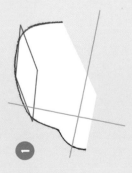

3

4

5

6

7

8

Scooter

☆ Gondola ☆

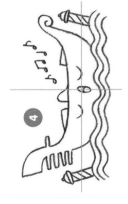

Sailing Boat

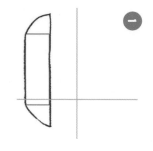

☆ Pirate Ship ☆

1

2

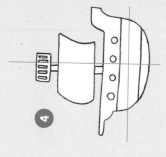

3

4

5

6

7

8

9

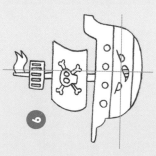

☆ Cruise Ship ☆

1

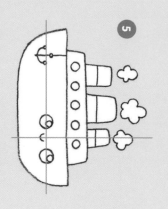

2

6

3

4

5

8

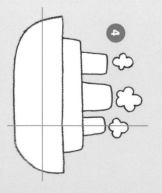

7

Submarine ☆

1

2

3

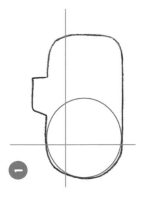

4

5

6

7

8

Desert Island ☆ ☆

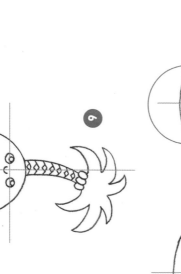

1

2

3

4

5

6

7

8

9

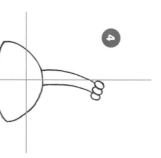

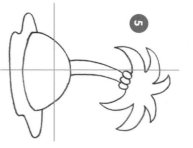

☆ Tepee ☆

☆ Circus Tent ☆

1

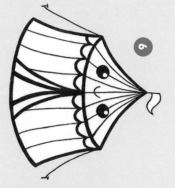

2

3

4

5

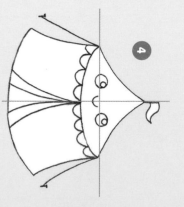

6

7

8

Windmill

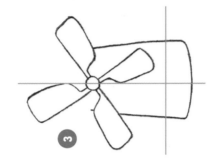

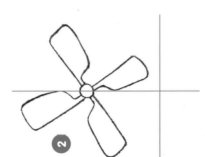

☆ **House** ☆

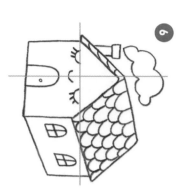

☆ Castle ☆

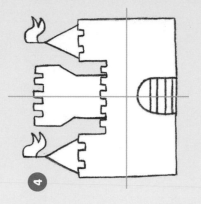

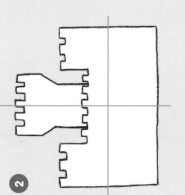

350

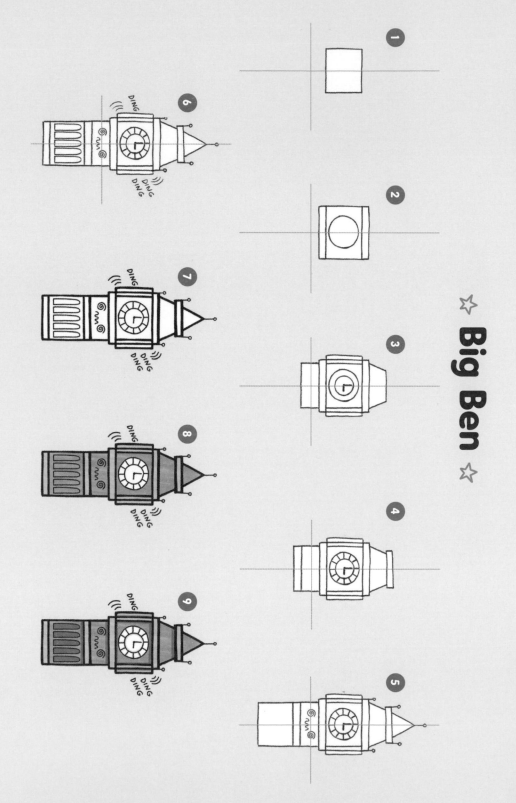

☆ **Big Ben** ☆

Leaning Tower of Pisa

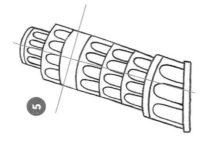

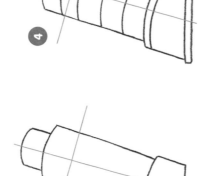

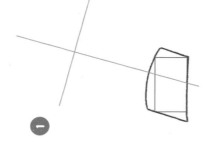

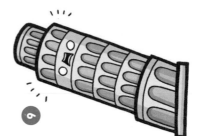

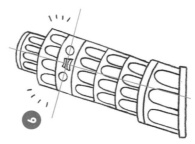

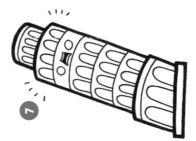

Eiffel Tower

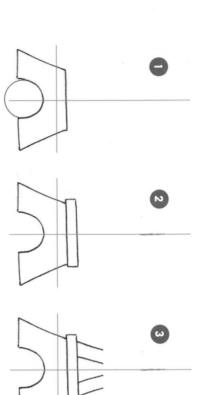

1

2

3

4

5

6

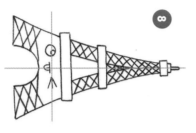

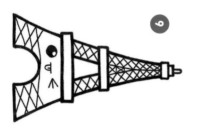

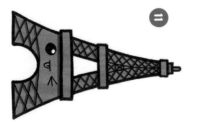

7

8

9

10

11

☆ Statue of Liberty ☆

1

2

3

4

5

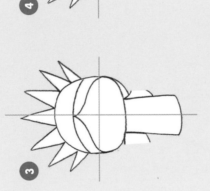

6

7

8

9

☆ Pyramids ☆

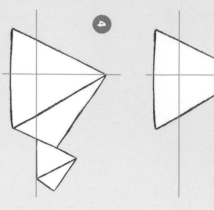

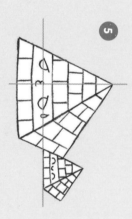

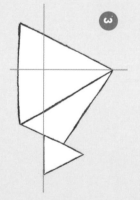

Sun

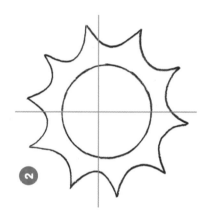

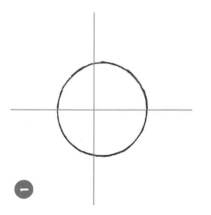

Sun, Clouds and Rainbow

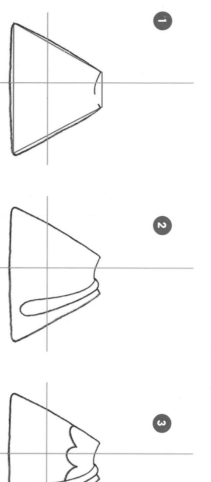

Volcano ☆

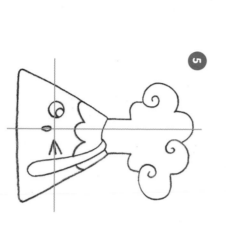

Fire ☆ ☆

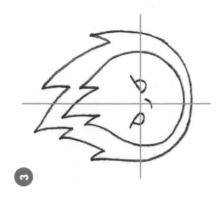

3

6

2

5

1

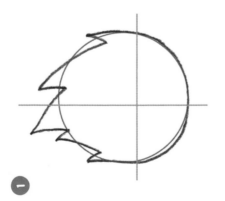

4

☆ Tornado ☆

☆ Rainclouds, Rain and Lightning ☆

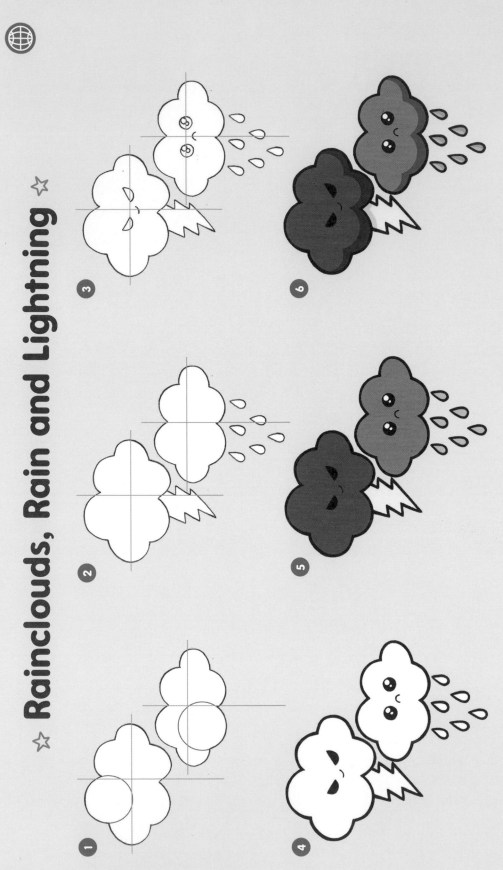

☆ Mountain ☆

1
2
3
4
5
6
7

☆ **Wave** ☆

3

2

1

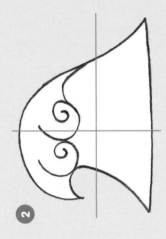

6

5

4

Water Droplet

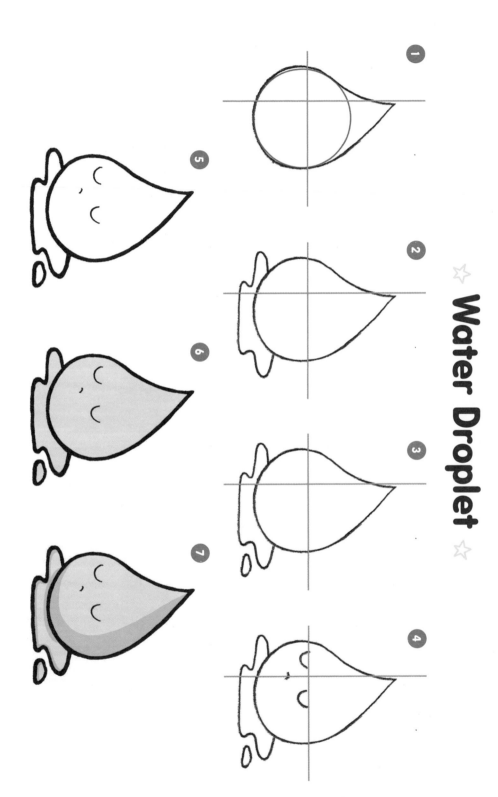

Earth ☆ ☆

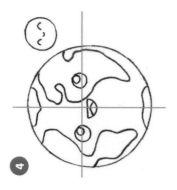

1

2

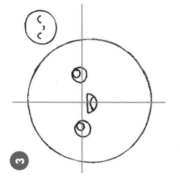

3

4

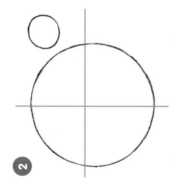

5

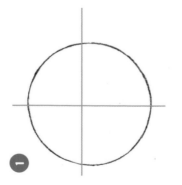

6

7

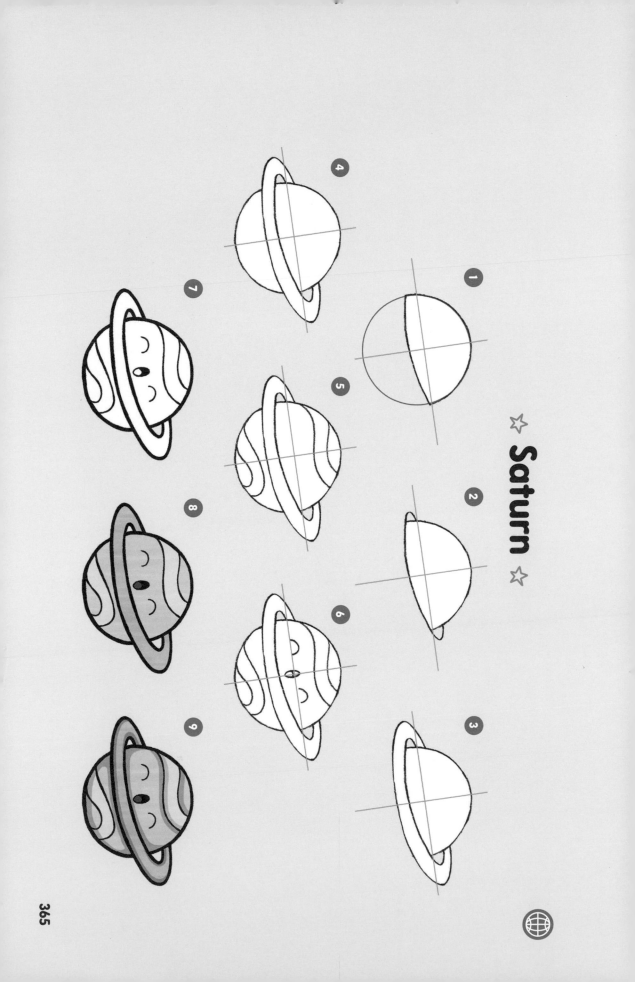

☆ Saturn ☆

365

☆ Meteor ☆

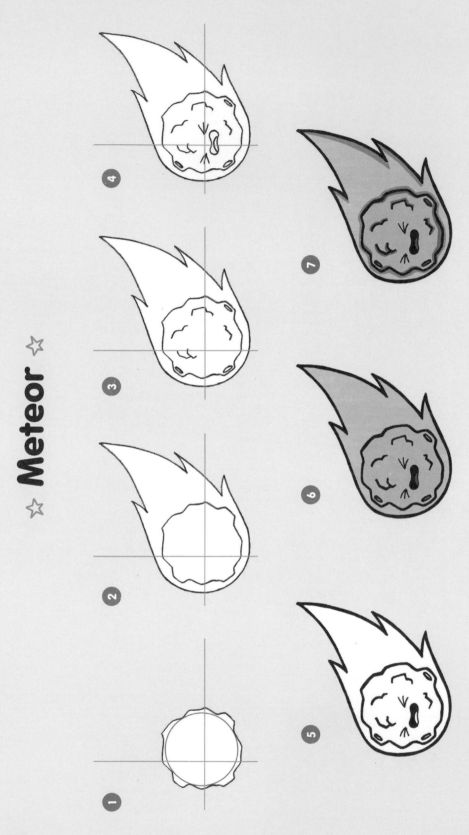

Shooting Star

Moon

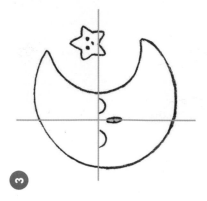

3

2

1

6

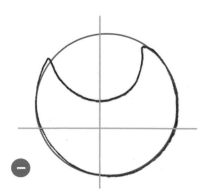

5

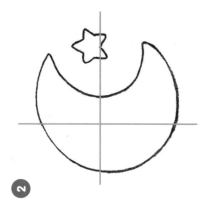

4